Twenty-First Century Presidential Elections

David A. Walker
John A. Largay Professor *Emeritus*
McDonough School of Business
Georgetown University
Washington, DC 20057
walkerd@georgetown.edu

Twenty-First Century Presidential Elections
Copyright © 2024 by North American Business Press, Inc.
ISBN: 978-1-948915-33-5

NORTH
AMERICAN BUSINESS
P R E S S

North American Business Press
Atlanta, Georgia
Miami, Florida
New York, New York
Toronto, Canada

FIRST PRINTING, JUNE 2024

FOR

AUDREY

MY INSPIRATION

FORWARD

Professor Ray Fair of Yale University lectured at Georgetown nearly the same time as I learned about the Iowa Electronic Market (IEM), developed by Robert Foresythe, my former student and co-author. The IEM shows how markets function and that maximizers' expectations dominate their preferences. The two approaches inspired the author's interest in forecasting U.S. presidential elections.

After publishing my early presidential popular and electoral college 2024 forecasts in The Journal of Forecasting in January 2023, my foolish pride motivated me to tabulate the differences between my actual results and forecasts in Table 1.1, which might encourage forecasters, political scientists, and sophisticated students to be more innovative than pollsters. This table contrasts differences between actual election results (a), Walker forecasts (w), and my errors (e) which follow:

2004: -1.1%;   2008: +1.8%;   2012: 0.8%;   2016: 0.6%; and 2020: 0.5%;   2024: ???.

The mean error is 0.5 percent, and the median error is 0.6 percent.

The monograph is a result of major editing of the author's previous papers and delineating the context of each election. Presidential election results change in only seven states. The other 43 states' history and one or two major new issues for a particular year determine the state's popular vote.

The monograph was completed on July 22. Sections Immeasureables and Unpredictables and Conclusions for Chapter 7 were revised in the third week of July.

ACKNOWLEDGEMENTS

Professors Keith Ord and Stan Nollan identified assumptions in drafts that would misinterpret results. Thank you to instructors who discussed issues that became part of the monograph, especially the late Ronald Koot, Tom Iwand, Karl Fox, Jati Sengupta, and Richard Upjohn. Research colleagues Reena Aggarwal, Bill Droms, Bill Novelli, Annette Shelby, Greg Squires, and Jay Wright provided useful suggestions.

Georgetown student research assistants supported my work across 25 years. Six (+) became co-authors. John Antonelli, Elizabeth Chant (+), Perry Rogers Comenos, Reilly Davis (+), Max Gaby (+), Joshua Goldstein (+), Christine Hunt (+), Eric Schwartz, Katie I. Smith (+), Kait Margraff Stephens, Kirsten Jacobson Thibault, and Chloe Wallach.

Thank you to Taylor and Francis, John Wiley & Co., and De Guyter Publishing for permission to use materials from my publications in their scholarly journals. Thanks to Dr. Donald Smith, editor, and his colleagues at North American Business Press, for managing and expediting the monograph production in less than 60 days.

TABLE OF CONTENTS

"Twenty- First Century Presidential Elections"

Chapter 1. PROLOGUE

Presidential Election Year 2004

David A. Walker
John A. Largay Professor *Emeritus*
Georgetown University
walkerd@georgetown.edu
202-679-1740

CHAPTER 1

PROLOGUE

My interest in presidential elections began in 1948, at age 7, when I heard President Truman speak from a caboose as his campaign train passed through York, Pennsylvania. My family were all Democrats, so, of course, as the youngest, I cheered for Republican New York Governor Thomas Dewey. I had heard that Truman's main experience was as a haberdasher, whatever that was. Quite a few years later, I learned that a haberdasher was someone who sold men's hats and clothing. Later, I learned that my family had been haberdashers since 1893.

On election night, my father convinced me to celebrate Dewey's victory, turn off the radio, and go to bed. I learned a valuable lesson and adopted Winston Churchill's motto: "Never, Never, Never Give Up."

Forecasters thought they had experienced even possible election result, when the 2000 election was decided in favor of George W. Bush by the Supreme Court just before Christmas on the basis of 527 votes in Florida. Then the 9/11 tragedy occurred killing 3,000 people and leaving a terrible feeling about fairness and safety across a 10 month period. Why would anyone try to forecast other 21st century presidential elections?

INTRODUCTION

Forecasting Elections

My first sophisticated exposure to forecasting presidential popular votes occurred in 1980 when I attended a lecture at Georgetown University by Professor Ray Fair from Yale. Professor Fair presented his economic model to predict the popular vote (Fair 1978). In addition, I was fascinated by Robert Forsythe's approach to developing the Iowa Electronic Market. Fair's consistent theme for 45 years has been that the election year performance of the economy determines the winner of the November presidential election. As I became more familiar with their work and others, my reaction was that one or two additional considerations, but not many, were needed to predict each presidential election.

President Biden's re-election was expected to depend on independent voters and reactions to Supreme Court rulings since 2020 (Walker, 2023). Potential voters (Zitner, 2024) were beginning to appreciate the Biden Administration's commitments and success to strengthen the U.S. economy By August 1, he was an afterthought as a candidate.

Since the presidential election of 2004, the author has analyzed each presidential election and published a research paper predicting the result. The six elections are the subjects of Chapters 2-7 in the monograph (see Table of Contents). An extended model is re-estimated each election year to include a unique circumstance beyond Fair's fundamental model. For 2008 and 2012, the forecast equation is enhanced to represent aspects of the financial crisis. As the nominating process became more public with open primaries and fewer Super Delegates, unity for the party not occupying the White House has become important.

MODEL DEVELOPMENT

Ray Fair developed models to represent a range of economic and policy issues. In his book (Fair, 2002) on predictive modeling, he discusses his approach to model building and how polls can be wrong because samples were not representative of the population. Dewey did not beat Truman in 1948. In 1936, the Literary Digest polled only wealthy potential voters with telephones and concluded that Alf Landon would beat the incumbent, Franklin Delano Roosevelt.

Fair delineates his approach to modeling in seven stages (Fair, 2002, Ch. 2). His stages (paraphrased) follow:

Stages of Modeling

1. Start with an understanding of your forecast goal.
2. Review the relevant literature and existing theories.

3. Sketch your ideas to develop your theory or model.
4. Identify what is unique about your theory or model.
5. Review existing data you can employ for your analysis.
6. Identify what new data you will need to collect.
7. Represent the data with a model (equation, picture, graph,or sketch)
8. Select useful quantitative tools and measures you will apply
9. Recognize limitations of your theory and/or model.
10. Develop your results and conclusions.
11. Test your theory and/or model.
12. Identify limitations and weaknesses of the model
13. CCompare your model/results with what is already known
14. Apply and communicate your results.

Fair warns model builders to be flexible in interpreting outcomes and be prepared to revise or adjust their predictions as new data or additional factors and issues become relevant.

Unique Aspects of Recent Elections

Each chapter of the monograph focuses on one election and recognizes unique issues for that presidential election. For 2004, following 9/11, a conservative incumbent had some advantage over a liberal Senator who had protested against the Vietnam War. In 2008, the country faced the most serious financial crisis since the Depression. Following eight years of Republican leadership, Barack Obama had an advantage with ideas as a new young Democratic candidate. By 2012, the Obama Administration had shown some success in dealing with the crisis, and many voters had remained committed to the incumbent. In 2016, Hillary Clinton (Obama's Secretary of State) was viewed as a mere extension of eight successful years of the Obama Administration. The Clinton campaign made some strategic mistakes, hardly campaigning in Michigan, allowing former President Bill Clinton to appear to intercede with the Attorney General concerning Secretary Clinton's handling of her government email account and her giving private lectures to a single investment bank to fund her family foundation. She opposed a first-time candidate, a former

3

television showman, and a New York real estate tycoon, with a unique approach to campaigning against other candidates and no political record to critique.

Almost twenty-five years after attending Fair's lecture, I reread Fair's 1978 paper and visited the Iowa Electronic Market. I thought a lecture on the two topics might encourage students to register and vote. My outstanding summer research assistant discovered that Fair made his 1920-2016 dataset and his approach to election forecasting available on his public website.

FAIR'S POPULAR VOTE MODEL

In his seminal paper, Fair (1978) recognized Kramer (1971) and Stigler (1973) for some of his interest in testing economic variables to predict presidential elections. Kramer's focus was unemployment and real economic growth. Stigler's survey showed that high inflation had a negative effect on an incumbent's re-election prospects. Inflation and women's choice are the key variables in the author's (2023) forecast for the 2024 presidential election.

Fair's model is creative and captures the essence of the U.S. economy across decades of presidential elections. His model, equation (F) below, is a multi-regression model, estimated under the usual assumptions and maintained on Professor Fair's website.

The numbers in parentheses ( ) are the t-statistics for the coefficients directly above the t-statistics. Each coefficient is statistically different from zero at the 5 percent probability level or less, except for the coefficient of WAR (discussed below). The coefficient of WAR is not different from zero at a meaningful probability level. Fair's independent variables are defined in the appendix to this chapter. V is the popular vote for a presidential election.

$$V = 48.70 - .78\ \text{INFL} + 0.65\ \text{GR} + 0.94\ \text{GDNES} + 3.23\ \text{PERSON} - 3.06\ \text{DUR}$$
$$(18.91)\quad (-2.86)\qquad (6.72)\qquad (3.59)\qquad\qquad (2.72)\qquad\qquad (-2.76)$$

$$- 2.42\ \text{PARTY} + 3.46\ \text{WAR} \quad \overline{R^2} = .90 \quad F = 26.93 \quad DW = 2.81$$
$$(-4.50)\qquad\qquad (1.56)$$

[F]

The measures of the quality of the Fair model are the adjusted R-square (percentage of variance in V that the model explains), the F-statistic (a measure for goodness of fit for the linear model), and the Durban-Watson (D.W.) statistic, which measure the auto-correlation among the error terms. The adjusted R-square accounts for the model's explained variance with attention to the small number of elections for which there are data. The D.W., 0 < D.W. < 4, far from 2.0, suggests auto-correlation among the errors from one election to the next. Details are discussed in the next chapter, where the Walker model has a D.W. much closer to 2.0, and the model is adjusted for auto-correlation.

For the Fair model, the adjusted R2 is high (near its limit of 1.00). The F-statistic is statistically significant at any meaningful probability level. The high D.W. (2.81) indicates that the Fair model has auto-correlated error terms.

Coefficients

The numerical values of the coefficients in Fair's model deserve particular attention. The coefficient of WAR is not statistically significant at even the 10 percent probability level. Therefore, the relevance of whether the country is at war should have limited statistical influence on Fair's forecast for V.

Incumbency, represented by PERSON and PARTY is important. If a candidate is running for a second term, their joint impact on the popular vote, V, is 3.23 percent. The effect is much smaller than if the incumbent's party is already serving a second term, less than one-quarter of one percent, 0.17. When FDR ran for a third term, the effect on V was negative and reduced his predicted popular vote. (-0.59 = 3.23 – 3.82). If the candidate is a Democrat, as Roosevelt, the comparable aggregate coefficients are +0.81 (3.23 – 2.42), -2.25 (0.17 – 2.42), and – 3.01 (-0.59 – 2.42). (Chapter 7 provides considerably more discussion of incumbency.)

A Republican incumbent has a distinct advantage in the popular vote race, according to the model. The Republican has almost a two-and-a-half percent increase (+2.42) in the popular vote.

The coefficients of the major economic factors -- the impact of per capita growth (GR) +0.65 and inflation (INFL) -0.78 -- are numerically important. For a one percent increase in inflation and the same increase in per capita GDP, the effect on the popular vote, V, is -0.13.

Fair's Assumptions

Fair made three implicit assumptions, (1F), (2F), and (3F), developing his model. These assumptions reduce the power of his forecasts. Modifying these assumptions enhances his model, which is the subject of Chapter Two.

(1F) Fair excludes the Korean and Viet Nam years from his classification of war election years. General Dwight Eisenhower, the highly decorated World War II leader, won the presidential election of 1952. He convinced Americans he could settle the Korean War by going to Korea to meet with the Korean generals. In fact, the Korean War had virtually ended by Eisenhower's inauguration day.

Incumbent Lyndon Johnson withdrew as a candidate for a second term in March 1968 because he was blamed for failing to control the U.S. military performance in Vietnam when the Administration had provided infinite resources. He had won his first term in 1964 in a landslide. He was correctly credited with enacting the Voting Rights legislation (with the assistance of his long-time Southern Senate colleagues), proposed by President Kennedy before his assassination, and initiating effective domestic programs such as Head Start.

(2F) Fair's assessment of the U.S. economy caused him to link three of his key variables. During the years that he coded as war election years (WAR = 1), he assigned values of 0 for GOODNEWS and INFLATION during war years.

The Vietnam War was a case in which Fair's coding was not appropriate. During the war, the Johnson Administration foolishly insisted the U.S. could afford "guns and butter" and that a tax increase was not necessary.

(3F) Fair chose not remove autocorrelation from his model. He explained (in a private meeting) that presidential elections four years apart is long enough not to be concerned with auto-correlated errors. Successive presidential elections are adjoining observations; often a party nominates the same candidate, as an incumbent, from the previous election. Ali Stevenson was the Democratic nominee in 1952 and 1956, but not an incumbent.

Fair's model became the foundation for the author to develop an enhanced model (W), which is the subject of chapter 2.

David A. Walker

TABLE 1.1: UNIQUE ELECTION ISSUES AND FORECASTS

ELECTION YEAR	DEMOCRAT REPUBLICAN	POPULAR ACTUAL% (a) WALKER (w)	ELECTORAL COLLEGE	UNIQUE ISSUE
2024	Harris TRUMP	50.4 w revised	274 w	Choose Incumbency
2024	BIDEN TRUMP	53.7 w	272 w	HOUSE control
2020	BIDEN* TRUMP	52.7 r 52.2 w 0.5% e	301 w 306 r	HOUSE control
2016	H. CLINTON TRUMP *	51.1 r 50.5 w 0.6 % e	306 a	probit state-state EC model & forecast
2012	OBAMA * ROOMNEY	51.9 r 51.1 w 0.8% e	332 a	% ΔDJ e^{rT}
2008	OBAMA* McCAIN	53.4 r 51.6 w 1.8 % e	365	macro model % ΔDJ * T increasing impact
2004	BUSH* KERRY	51.2 r 52.3 w -1.1 % e	286	AR(1), DW WARS: Korea, Vietnam

e = a – w forecast error   a = actual vote recorded   w = walker forecast   EC = Electoral College
ERRORS 2024 ? 2020 0.5% 2016 0.6% 2012 0.8% 2008 1.8% 2004 -1.1%
MEAN=0.5% MED= 0.8% 16-24: 0.6

Definition of FAIR'S Variables

VOTE = the incumbent share of the two-party presidential vote.

GR = per capita election year GDP growth rate in quarters1-3.

INFL = absolute value of growth rate of GDP deflator in the first 15 quarters of the administration, except for 1920, 1944, and 1948, where values are zero.
INFL = 0 for 1920, 1944, 1948, 1952, 1968, and 1972.

GDNES = quarters of the first 15 quarters of an administration when real per capita GDP growth > 3.2 annual %, but 1920, 1944, and 1948, values =0

GDNES = 0 for 1920, 1944, 1948, 1952, 1968, and 1972.

PERSON = 1 if the incumbent is running for re-election, and 0 otherwise.

DUR = 0 if the incumbent party is in power for 1 term, 1 if the incumbent is in power for 2 consecutive terms, 1.25 if incumbent is in power for 3 consecutive terms.

PARTY= 1 if there is a Democratic incumbent at the time of the election and -1 if there is a Republican incumbent.

WAR = 1 Fair for 1920, 1944, and 1948, and 0 otherwise.
Walker expanded the list to include 1952, 1968, and 1972 for WAR = 1.

CHAPTER 2

AN ENHANCED MODEL : ELECTION 2004[1]

After attending Professor Ray Fair's 1980 Georgetown lecture and reading his research over many years, I enhanced Fair's model by loosening three implicit assumptions (1F, 2F, and 3F, in Chapter One). I gathered additional data and applied a well-known statistical adjustment to the error terms.

(1) Coding 1952, 1964, 1968, 2004, 2008, and 2012 as WAR election years.
(2) Replacing 0 values for GDNES and INFL with data during war years.
(3) Applying a standard time-series AR(1) correction to remove autocorrelation from the error terms

Contrasting Two Models

The Fair model is innovative and effective. By enhancing it, the popular vote forecast should have smaller errors. In addition, for each election beginning in 2004, one **critical**, unique issue is represented by constructing a new independent variable and including it in the model. The enhanced model is Equation [W], the Walker model. The variables are defined on the last page of this chapter.

$$V = 46.19 - .70\,INFL + 0.67\,GR + 1.18\,GDNES + 2.42\,INCUMBENT - 1.29\,DUR$$
$$\quad (28.77) \quad (-4.30) \quad (10.28) \quad (7.23) \quad (2.13) \quad (-1.67)$$
$$\text{[W]}$$

---

[1] This chapter is developed from "Predicting Presidential Eletion Results" published in APPLIED ECONOMICS in March 20. The author thanks Taylor & Francis for their permission to use that material.

- 2.65 PARTY +5.20 WAR   -0.73 AR(1) R^2 =.94, F = 41.21, DW = 2.27
   (-7.13)   (3.95)   (-3.76)

For comparison, the Fair model, [F], is repeated from Chapter One.

V = 48.70 - .78 INFL + 0.65 GR + 0.94 GDNES + 3.23 PERSON - 3.06 DUR
   (18.91) (-2.86)   (6.72)   (3.59)   (2.72)   (-2.76)

   - 2.42 PARTY + 3.46 WAR $\overline{R^2}$ = .90   F = 26.93   DW = 2.81
      (-4.50)   (1.56*

[F]

This chapter is developed from "Predicting Presidential Eletion Results" published in APPLIED ECONOMICS in March 20. The author thanks Taylor & Francis for their permission to use that material.

There is universal agreement that the economy's performance during a presidential election year is a critical determinant of a national election. Fair accounted for FDR winning four elections by including DURATION (DUR) in his model. The 22nd Amendment to the Constitution, enacted in 1951, restricts a person from serving more than two four-year terms as president. Fair's variable PERSON is renamed INCUMBENT in [W].

The coefficients of the three economic variables – INFL, GR, and GDNES – each have a larger t-statistic in [W] than in [F]. Adjusting for the three implicit assumptions provides [W], which is statistically stronger than [F]. The difference between the adjusted R squared is only 0.04, but the difference between the F statistics is quite large: 14.28 (41.21 – 26.93).

Removing the auto-correlation, (3) above, adjusts for auto-correlated error terms from one presidential election to the next. The Durbin-Watson statistic in [W] is 2.27, signaling less auto-correlation than [F] for a model with seven independent variables. For model [F], the DW is 2.81, which is outside the range of 0.60 to 2.34. A Durbin-Watson inside the range would allow a conclusion of no further auto-correlation among the errors in [F]. The hypothesis that [W] does not have auto-correlated errors can be accepted at the 5 percent probability level.

[W] is statistically superior to [F]. Numbers in parentheses are t-statistics for their respective coefficients. Including Korea and Vietnam, as WAR presidential election years, increased the coefficient of WAR and raised its t-statistic from 1.56 to 3.95, which is statistically significant at the .001 level. The low but statistically significant t-statistics for INCUMBENCY in [W] and PERSON in [F] result from including PARTY in each model, which may absorb some of the significance of INCUMBENCY. INCUMBENCY is explored further in Chapter 7.

The Iowa Electronic Market: A "Poll" Alternative to Models

In contrast to models and polls, different approaches have been created to forecast presidential elections and observe voters' plans close to Election Day. Forty years ago, the Iowa Electronic Market (IEM) was developed at the University of Iowa as a research and teaching tool to understand the fundamentals of futures markets. The IEM provides a contrasting approach to predicting elections (Berg et al., 2004). Participants are optimizing their personal dollar utilities in a market-based system.

The IEM predicts presidential election results under the regulatory purview of the Commodities Futures Trading Commission. An investor may open an account with a maximum of $500 to buy and sell political candidates' futures contracts (shares) over the Internet.

The IEM was developed, with support from the National Science Foundation, the U.S. Department of Education, and other public and private sector sponsors, to broaden the public understanding of how a market operates. As a research tool, the IEM has increased understanding of how financial markets operate as they apply to political and economic events.

Forsythe and his colleagues (1992, 1998) argue that restricting "investors" to a maximum account of $500 does not reduce the IEM's ability to predict outcomes. Because "investors" commit their own funds, they reflect what they expect to occur without the biases of their personal preferences, philosophical inclinations, or party affiliations.

Share prices are based on what percentage of the two-party vote an investor expects each candidate to receive on Election Day. Comparing the IEM's forecast on election eve with final expert polls, the IEM has forecasted presidential vote shares more accurately than the majority of pollsters for many national, state, and foreign elections.

9/11 2001 AND THE IRAQ WAR

For the presidential election in 2004, 9/11 and the Iraq invasion were still affecting voters decisions. Recall that Al-Qaeda terrorists hijacked American airplanes and crashed them into three high-rise office buildings in lower Manhattan of New York City and the Pentagon in Washington. Courageous passengers on a plane that departed from Washington Dulles Airport prevented the terrorists from bombing the White House. The American public and politicians from both parties demanded that the George W. Bush Administration implement a vigorous military response.

In his January 2002 State of the Union Address, President Bush assured the country he was focused on the Middle East but that it would require much of 2002 to prepare an appropriate military response. On October 2, 2002, the Congress approved a war against Iraq.

The American intelligence on the Middle East was highly flawed. The Bush Administration and eighty-five percent of Americans became convinced that Iraq had supported Al-Qaeda terrorists for 9/11 and that Iraq President Saddam Hussain had developed weapons of mass destruction to attack the United States (*Encyclopedia Britannica,* 2024).

In the spring of 2003, U.S. and British forces invaded Iraq and defeated Iraqi military forces. One thousand American and British servicemen and women were lost. Saddam was captured on December 13, 2003, and convicted of crimes against humanity by an Iraqi Special Tribunal. He was executed on December 30, 2006, after Bush had been inaugurated for his second term. The War continued for five more years until 2011. The 2003 Iraq invasion and eight more years of war were controversial. France, Germany, and New Zealand were not confident of American intelligence and opposed the invasion of Iraq. Forty-seven members of the U.S. Senate (45 Democrats, plus Republicans Grassley (IA) and Hatfield (OR)) opposed the war. In July 2003, President Bush appointed a Commission to study 9/11. In July 2004, the Commission reported that Saddam Hussain did not have weapons of mass destruction and that there was no direct link between the 9/11 terrorist attacks and the Iraqi government.

The country would be at war throughout Bush's second term, 2005 – 2009. Barak Obama was one of the Senators who opposed the war. By 2008, the financial crisis had become another critical issue.

THE CANDIDATES

Election Choice

Voters' choice in November 2004 was between the incumbent, Texas Republican, who entered office in 2001, expecting to focus on domestic issues, and Senator John Kerry, a liberal Democrat representing Massachusetts in the Senate. The president would begin his term in 2005 dealing with the 9/11 Commission Report that concluded Iraq did not have the capability of attacking the U.S.

George W. Bush

George W. Bush was inaugurated as president in January 2001, only nine years after his father, George H.W. Bush, had been defeated for re-election by Bill Clinton. George W. served as his father's campaign manager in 1992, seeking a second term, and learned a great deal about how an incumbent should run for re-election.

George W. Bush had only served one term as Governor of the State of Texas (1996-2000) when he became a presidential candidate. He had been a businessman, rancher, and part owner of the Houston Texas Rangers major league baseball team. Since their marriage, the Governor has credited his wife, Laura, for giving him good advice and stabilizing his personal life. His military experience was through weekend drills as a member of the Texas National Guard, from which he received a six-month leave of absence to campaign for governor.

George W's major agenda as Governor was to improve the educational system in Texas. He had learned about the issues from Laura, a second-grade teacher and a librarian. In 1978, he had been defeated for a seat in the House of Representatives. He campaigned on his personal experience and regional issues facing Texas and the Southwest. He did not show much interest in international affairs or global conflicts. He was defeated by Democrat James Vance.

George W's choice for his running mate in 2001 was Richard Cheney, who was a well-known conservative with many years of Washington experience. Cheney brought balance to the Republican ticket. He had served as Secretary of Defense for President George H. W. Bush and as White House Chief of Staff for President Gerald Ford after Nixon's resignation. For the next ten years, he was the only member of the House of Representatives representing Wyoming.

Bush brought the same experience to the White House as any first-term President who was a one-term governor. Only nine months after his inauguration, he was faced with the tragic Al-Qaeda attacks on New York City and Washington. In 2004, campaigning for re-election, Bush had the benefits of any incumbent. He began campaigning in the White House and had a team of loyal surrogates from the Cabinet who served at the President's pleasure.

John F. Kerry

John Kerry, the Democratic candidate, is the son of a military pilot. After graduating from college, he enlisted in the Navy. He was selected for Officers Candidate School and was commissioned as a second lieutenant. Kerry was sent to Vietnam to command a Swift Boat crew. He served four years in Vietnam and was awarded numerous medals, including the Purple Heart for bravery and leadership. Upon his discharge, Kerry became a war protester and an active member of Vietnam Veterans Against the War (VVAW).

Kerry won his first Senate seat in 1984 and served five terms. In 29 years, Kerry never sponsored any major legislation. In the last year of his fifth term, President Obama appointed him Secretary of State, following Hillary Clinton's service.

Kerry lost a close election to incumbent Bush. He received 49.3 percent of the popular vote and 252 Electoral Votes. His decision to protest the war offended many voters who were selecting a president to deal with the compromised U.S. intelligence system, terrorists, the war in Iraq, and plans to reconstruct three New York skyscrapers and the Pentagon.

2004 [W] FORECASTS

Election Environment for [W]

Applying the enhanced model to predict the 2004 election was challenging, only six months after the release of the 9/11 Commission Report. INCUMBENT and PARTY are binary variables with coefficients of +2.42 and -2.65, respectively. Both coefficients are statistically different from zero at the 5 percent probability level. A Republican incumbent has the arithmetic contribution to the popular vote forecast of 5.07 percent (2.42 * 1.0 + -2.65 * (-1.0)).

2004 Election Results

The Bush-Cheney team received 50.7 percent of the popular vote and 286 electoral votes, only 18 more than necessary to be re-elected. The enhanced Walker model prediction was that the incumbent party would receive 52.3 percent of the popular vote with an error of 0.9 percent. The 0.9 percent error was not large compared to the alternative forecasts in Table 2.1. The enhancement of the Fair model was beneficial.

The table contrasts Bush's actual share of the major two-party votes with forecasts from the Fair model, the Walker model, the IEM closing price, and predictions by five highly regarded political scientists. Fair posted input data on his website to apply his model to predict the vote share for incumbent President Bush.

Absolute Forecast Errors

Table 2.2 contrasts the absolute values of the prediction errors for 1924–2004 for the Fair and Walker models. Contrasting absolute values prevents positive and negative errors from offsetting each other.

Polls and Models

Some analysts and experts prefer to rely on polls rather than models. There is always the difficulty of knowing who will vote. Neither the polls nor models can take account of the weather on Election Day and other surprising events immediately before the election.

For some years, polls have been quite accurate, but not always. For example, the erroneous polls in 2016 were attributed to voters unwilling to discuss their voting plans (Baltz, 2021).

Most polling data can be accumulated almost immediately before Election Day. With technology and more sophisticated polling, polls should become more accurate over time. Most major media sources complete their polls the weekend before Election Day and sometimes capture trends that models do not identify.

CONCLUSIONS

Macro Conclusions

Political scientists and the Media have found that most years' polls and/or presidential satisfaction data gathered shortly before a presidential election are effective predictors of presidential elections. Forecasts that rely heavily on polls incur the risks of sampling error and biased responses according to how questions are formulated. The IEM should have consistent success in predicting the popular vote elections because investors are using their own money, although the dollar amounts are small.

The modelers who depend on economic data usually do not have the most current data, and they depend on a small number of presidential elections, some of which are so long ago that they may be irrelevant.

Model W Conclusions

Walker's 2004 election forecast provides a more accurate forecast than Fair's prediction. The [W] forecast has a 0.9 percent error, which is tied for the lowest error with the prediction by well-known political scientists Wlezien and Erikson in Table 2.1. The Walker model has mean and median errors that are approximately 70 percent of the Fair model average errors, and the Walker model has a much smaller standard error. The Walker model has a considerably lower average forecast error, a smaller standard error of the estimate, stronger aggregate model test statistics, and higher degrees of difference from zero for the coefficients of individual explanatory variables.

Table 2.1 2004 Election Results and Forecasts

Forecast	G. W. Bush Vote Share	Date	Actual - Forecast
Actual Vote	51.4	11/29/04	-
Fair Model	57.7	11/1/04	+6.3
Walker	52.3	11/1/04	+0.9
IEM	50.4	11/1/04	-1.0
*Lewis-Beck/Tien	49.9	8/27/04	-1.5
*Wlezien/Erikson	52.3	8/27/04	+0.9
*Hibbs	53.0	7/26/04	+1.6
*Abramowitz	53.7	7/3/04	+2.3
*Campbell	53.8	9/6/04	+2.4

**Table 2.2 Absolute Values of Prediction Errors:
Vote – Predicted Vote 1924 - 2004**

Measure	Fair Model	Walker
MEAN	1.68	1.19
MEDIAN	1.27	0.94
MAXIMUM	6.29	3.84
MINIMUM	0.05	0.003
STAND. DEV.	1.56	0.81

David A. Walker

Definition of WALKER'S Variables

VOTE = the incumbent share of the two-party presidential vote.

INFL = absolute value of growth rate of GDP deflator in the first 15 quarters of an administration, collected data for 1920, 1944, 1948, 1952, 1968, 1972, and all future presidential elections.

GR = per capita election year GDP growth rate in quarters1-3.

GDNES = quarters of the first 15 quarters of an administration when real per capita GDP growth > 3.2 annual %, collected data for 1920, 1944, 1948, 1952, 1968, 1972, and all future elections.

INCUMBENT (labeled PERSON by Fair) = 1 if the incumbent is running for re-election, and 0 otherwise.

DUR = 0 if the incumbent party is in power for 1 term, 1 if the incumbent is in power for 2 consecutive terms, 1.25 if incumbent is in power for 3 consecutive terms.

PARTY= 1 if there is a Democratic incumbent at the time of the election and -1 if there is a Republican incumbent.

WAR = 1 for 1920, 1944, 1948, 1952, 1968, 1972, 2004, 2008, 2012, and 0 otherwise.

20

CHAPTER 3

ELECTION 2008 : BARACK OBAMA <u>VS</u> JOHN McCAIN[2]

BACKGROUND

The first two chapters delineated Fair's fundamental model (F) and the author's enhancement (W). The enhancement adjusts for Fair's three implicit assumptions, but it could only be estimated with 21 observations. Collecting data for later elections and coding the 2004 and 2008 elections as war election years had expanded the database.

The first Bush Administration term had begun at a peaceful time, with a fiscal surplus from the Clinton Administration, possibilities for tax cuts, and the election of a Texas Governor who planned to focus on education and domestic issues. The second George W. Bush Administration concluded with a large fiscal deficit, the greatest financial crisis the nation had faced since the 1930s, and the war in Iraq that did not end until 2013. By 2008, voters were ready to elect a young president who brought new ideas to the White House to deal with the financial crisis and the war in Iraq.

THE CANDIDATES

Barack Obama, the first African-American president, had only four years of national experience as a U.S. Senator from Illinois. His

[2] This chapter is developed from "Presidential Election Forecasts" published in THE FORUM in December 2008. The author thanks DeGruyter Publishing Company for their permission to use that material.

opponent was John McCain, a Republican Arizona Senator, who sought the Republican nomination in 2000 and 2004.

Barack Obama

Barack Obama was virtually unknown until he gave a dynamic speech at the 2004 Democratic convention. Obama was 44 years old. He had served as an Illinois state senator from south Chicago. Hillary Clinton was expected to be the Democratic nominee after competing against five men. Obama continued to oppose her in the primaries and ranked second, accumulating a significant number of delegates. In those races, Mrs. Clinton won 100,000 more popular votes and more delegates than Obama; however, he gained strong support from the party's Super Delegates, who dominated the decision and chose him to be the Democrat nominee at the national convention.

Obama's father was an African from Kenya who came to study in Hawaii and married his mother, a white woman from Kansas. They settled in Hawaii, where Obama was born and raised by his mother and grandparents. Obama's father moved from Hawaii to Boston to study at Harvard without the family and then returned to Kenya. Donald Trump accused Obama of being ineligible to run for president until Obama released his birth certificate.

Obama began his collegiate studies at Occidental College in California. After one year, he was dissatisfied with the intellectual environment and moved to Columbia University in New York through a transfer program arranged between the two colleges. Obama continued to Harvard Law School, graduated with high honors, and served as head of *Harvard's Law Review*.

Obama chose Senator Joe Biden as his running mate. Biden was serving his 6th term in the Senate from Delaware and had served 12 years on the Senate Foreign Relations Committee. He was a popular Senator, will-liked by party elders, and a liberal Catholic. He brought a strong regional and philosophical balance to the ticket and provided the experience Obama lacked.

John McCain

The Republicans nominated 5-term U.S. Senator John McCain in 2008. He had vigorously opposed George W. Bush for the 2000

Republican nomination, winning the 2000 New Hampshire primary, but lost South Carolina in an ugly campaign against him and then lost 9 of 13 "Super Tuesday" primaries. McCain's Republican opponents developed an ugly campaign in South Carolina, claiming he had fathered an African American baby out of wedlock. In fact, the Senator and his wife had adopted a baby from Bangladesh after one of Mrs. McCain's numerous trips to South Asia. Mrs. McCain spent many years leading global efforts to provide food, clothing, and shelter for young children in the world's poorest countries. She became a global ambassador for her efforts in 2022.

McCain was a graduate of the US Naval Academy and had a career as a Navy pilot. He had been captured in Vietnam when his airplane was brought down by enemy fire. He was a decorated, abused war prisoner from 1967 to 1973 in Hanoi, at what he called the "Hanoi Hilton" prison camp. After his Navy career, McCain settled in Arizona and served two terms in the House of Representatives and 31 years in the Senate.

Throughout his extensive naval career, including his four years at the Naval Academy, John McCain was viewed as highly independent and somewhat of a maverick, refusing to follow rules or customs with which he disagreed. He was often protected by his father and grandfather, both of whom had been Navy Admirals. McCain, a lifelong Republican, later opposed Donald Trump throughout Trump's presidency. Years after the 2008 campaign, McCain left his deathbed and chartered a plane to travel from Arizona to the Senate to vote against Trump's effort to eliminate the Obamacare national health insurance program.

McCain chose first-term Alaska Governor Sarah Palin to be his vice-presidential candidate. She was only the second woman to be a vice-presidential candidate on for a major party national ticket. Supposedly, McCain had only met Palin once before he nominated her. Palin became known for her campaign gaffs. She addressed her lack of international experience by claiming, "I can see Russia from the front porch of my house" in Alaska.

In his memoir, McCain admitted that he had preferred to choose former Democratic Senator Joseph Lieberman, who had become an independent. McCain faced vigorous pressure from numerous top-level Republicans who refused to support a former Democrat on the Republican ticket. (Lieberman had run as Al Gore's vice-presidential candidate on the Democratic ticket in 2000.)

CAMPAIGN ISSUES

As they chose between Barack Obama and John McCain, 2008 presidential voters were deciding which candidate could manage two major issues: Ending the War in Iraq and solving the Financial Crisis. The two issues would occupy much of the new Administration's early years. Enacting national health insurance was at the top of President Obama's concern because the Democrats had control of both houses of Congress.

The impact of the financial crisis on the 2008 campaign was shown by the two candidates' interaction with President George W. Bush and his financial advisors at a White House October briefing for the candidates. Obama was actively engaged during the meeting, asking several detailed and important questions. McCain was quiet and did not ask significant questions or request data.

9/11 2001 and the Iraq War

The Iraq war continued through the first three years of the new Administration. By January 2009, Saddam Hussain had been executed, and the Commission on 9/11 Report was published, concluding there was no direct link between the 9/11 terrorist attacks and Saddam's government.

Financial Crisis of 2008

The domestic financial crisis, which the U.S. "exported" to many other countries, had fully emerged by March 2008, while the 2008 primaries were dominating candidates' campaigns and U.S. politics. On March 15, 2008, Bear Stearns, a major investment bank, failed. Federal financial regulators arranged for J.P. Morgan (JPM) to acquire the bank. JPM had done quite a lot of business with Bear Stearns for years and did not require much time to complete its due diligence to make an offer. JPM offered $2 per share of Bear Stearns stock, and there were no other qualified bidders. The regulators, including the Board of Governors of the Federal Reserve, the New York Federal Reserve Bank, the FDIC, and various divisions of the U.S. Treasury, approved the sale (Sorkin, 2018). Bear Stearns' shareholders challenged the $2 share price, which was renegotiated to $10 per share. The basis of the challenge was that just one of the Bear Stearns' buildings on Park Avenue in New York City that JPM acquired had been appraised above the offer of $2 per share times the number of JPM shares that Bear Stearns stockholders were offered.

On September 15, 2008, Lehman Brothers declared bankruptcy. The same day, Merrill Lynch went into bankruptcy, and Bank of America acquired it. Ten days later, with $1.9 billion in assets, the Washington Mutual Savings Bank declared bankruptcy and was acquired by JPM. Washington Mutual was the largest bank failure in U.S. history. The bank had focused on real estate lending throughout the West Coast. The crisis cost far more than the financial regulators could handle without Congressional action.

After Congressional hearings, the House of Representatives approved the Troubled Asset Relief Program (TARP) on September 30, 2008. The U.S. Treasury and Secretary Paulson proposed an alternative program. Instead of having the Treasury purchase toxic assets from hundreds of failing and weak institutions, their plan was for a weak institution to issue preferred stock in exchange for cash. The Treasury would hold the preferred stock until the institution was financially able to repurchase the stock. TARP would have required financial regulators to value all of the assets of weak banks and savings institutions, and the Treasury would purchase institutions' toxic assets. The simpler Paulson – Treasury plan was modified and included in the Economic Stabilization Program, enacted on October 3, 2008.

The weak institutions were expected to repurchase the stock from the Treasury within five years. The banks were required to pay a five percent dividend on the preferred stock during the five-year period. If an institution could not repurchase the preferred stock within five years, the dividend rate increased to nine percent as an incentive for banks to repurchase their stock before the end of five years. The great majority of the institutions were able to repurchase their preferred stock within the five-year period. The U.S. Treasury made a substantial profit from the program.

Weak institutions complained bitterly about the five-year provision. The regulators disagreed vigorously. The regulators informed the banks that five years was more than enough time to improve their operating conditions or find a merger partner.

Responsibility for the Crisis

There were a multitude of responsibilities for the crisis, but the most important cause was that banks and savings and loan associations were making mortgage loans to many borrowers who had few or no prospects of making the loan payments. Critics of the program called these "no doc loans" because the documentation and record keeping by the lenders were so inadequate.

Lending banks and savings institutions were satisfied to make the "no-doc loans" because they knew they would "securitize" their mortgage loans. Securitization allowed the institutions to sell mortgage loans to U.S. government agencies (Fannie Mae, Freddie Mac, and Ginnie Mae). Securitizing a loan removed a weak loan from the institution's balance sheet. In many cases, securitizing the loans was more profitable for the institutions than collecting the loans, including the interest due. Eventually, the three government agencies ran out of money and required federal funding to remain viable.

There was considerable corruption in this process because many lending institutions were not concerned with collecting these outstanding loans. The loans would only appear on an institution's balance sheet for a very short time until the loan was sold to a federal government agency.

Congress liberalized the lending process by encouraging bank lending to a much wider range of applicants than had been able to obtain mortgage loans in the past. Borrowers did not have to exhibit much ability to repay the loans. Between January 1, 2008 and December 31, 2012, 465 banks and savings institutions failed with total assets of $333.3 billion. During a typical year without a crisis, approximately 25 small banks would fail, but the usual solution was for another bank to acquire a failing institution.

To deal with longer-run financial issues and the causes of the crisis, the Obama Administration began enforcing the Dodd-Frank bill that had been signed into law on May 10, 2008. The Act included substantial new global capital requirements for insured banks and savings institutions. It also raised the deposit insurance limit to $250,000 to protect individuals, sole proprietors, and partnerships; created the Consumer Protection Bureau; required all insured institutions to have a "living will" to provide a plan in case the institution violated its new capital regulations (such as requiring capital $\geq$ 8% of total assets); reconfigured the Board of Directors of the FDIC; and imposed some of the separation between commercial and investment banks that had existed since 1933. Separation was required by the Glass-Steagall Act of 1933 to deal with banking during the Depression era. The American Bankers Association (2010) published a thorough summary of the Dodd-Frank Act.

Stock Market Measures

Numerous scholars (Malkiel, 2023) have argued that the stock market represents the dynamic performance of an economy and that changes in the stock market values indicate how an economy is likely to perform approximately six months later. This six-month time has become shorter as many more small and large investors have held at least part of their wealth, particularly their retirement funds, in equities. Many of these funds are diversified into index funds like the S&P 500.

The 2008 financial crisis was characterized by the Dow Jones Industrial Index (DJ) decline. The Dow Jones Index declined 61.2 percent from 12,263 to 7,609 between March 31, 2008 and March 31, 2009. Virtually every portfolio and most individual stocks followed the same pattern.

Extended Walker Model

A new variable is introduced into the Walker Model for 2008 to represent the aggregate U.S. economy's financial performance. The measure is the percentage change in the DJ (% Δ DJ) from

January 1 to October 31 of each presidential election year. To capture the trend over the length of Fair's database, % Δ DJ is multiplied by time, T, to generate increasing weights for each future election as more investors enter the market.

Δ% DJ * T, T = 1, 2,…22 is employed to capture the role of changes in equity markets across the database. The estimated model is the Walker Market Model (WM).

$$V = \begin{array}{l} 42.05 \\ (18.76) \end{array} \begin{array}{l} -0.86\ \text{INFL} \\ (-2.93) \end{array} + \begin{array}{l} 0.54\ \text{GR} \\ (4.85) \end{array} + \begin{array}{l} 1.57\ \text{GDNES} \\ (5.27) \end{array} + \begin{array}{l} 3.78\ \text{INCUMBENT} \\ (3.50) \end{array}$$

$$\begin{array}{l} -2.91\ \text{PARTY} \\ (-4.84) \end{array} + \begin{array}{l} 5.85\ \text{WAR} \\ (2.32) \end{array} + \begin{array}{l} 0.015\ \% \ \Delta\ \text{DJT} \\ (2.96) \end{array} \quad \bar{R}^2 = .89 \quad DW = 2.21 \quad F = 24.66$$

(WM)

with the coefficient's t-statistics in ( ) directly under each coefficient. The adjusted R-square, F statistic, and Durbin-Watson statistic are quite close to the statistics for [W] in Chapter 2.

To include the impact of the War in Iraq, WAR equals 1.0 for 2004 and 2008. The Durbin-Watson statistic for (WM) is 2.21, which is within the range to accept the null hypothesis that the model does not need an adjustment to remove auto-correlation. The new variable, % Δ DJ * T, with the time trend, takes account of potentially auto-correlated errors in (WM). The aggregate model has an adjusted R^2 of .89 with an F-statistic of 24.66.

To forecast V, the popular vote for the 2008 Democratic candidate, values of many of the independent variables are known before the election. Inputting these values into (WM) produces a reduced market model to:

$$V = 50.80 + .54\ GR + .345\ \% \ \Delta\ DJ * T$$

For 2008, T = 22, % Δ DJ = - 30, and GR = 0.22. The forecast for V is 51.4 percent.

Table 3.1 provides the forecast results for (WM) and several other forecasts.

Barack Obama won the 2008 presidential election by 6.4 percentage points over John McCain. The margin was larger than most predictions.

The forecasts for Real Clear Politics (RCP Average of 11 polls), the IEM, and Ray Fair's model were collected Sunday,

November 2. 2008 at noon. The RCP reported 50.4 for Obama, 43.7 for McCain, and 5.9 undecided. The 5.9 was allocated 50.4/ (50.4+43.7) for Obama and the rest for McCain.

Based on the actual vote share for President-elect Obama at noon on Friday, November 7, the RCP Average with the allocation and the Iowa Electronic Market had the smallest forecast error. Each of the forecasts in Table 3.1 has reasonably small errors. [WM] had the largest forecast error.

The 30-percent decrease in the Dow Jones between January I and October 31 of 2008 is twice as large as during any election year since the 1930s. A value so far outside the data range may explain the 1.8 percent error for the Walker Market Model.

CONCLUSIONS

For 2008, the Walker model is extended to a market model to reflect the impact of the financial crisis on the economy. The variable is the percentage change in the Dow Jones Industrial Average between January 1 and October 31 of the presidential election year. The measure is weighted by time to capture the continuing growth of investor participation in the market over the 22 election years that comprise the database.

The forecast from the Walker Market Model is that Barack Obama would receive 51.4 percent of the major two-party popular vote. The forecast was 1.8 percent below Obama's popular vote. Although this forecast error is not huge, it is larger than others cited in Table 3.1. The smallest error was the average of the Real Clear Politics Poll average of 11 polls, which had an error of only - 0.04 percent. The Iowa Electronic Market error of 0.2 percent is quite small, measured by traders' activity at noon on Election Day.

The first Obama Administration handled the financial crisis as well or better than any other administration probably would have. The only comparison with the 2008 – 2009 calamity was the 1929 – 1930 Depression. Some analysts argue that the only way the United States rebounded from the depression of the 1930s was through the economic benefits of War Production and military and civilian deployment and employment for the Allies in World War II.

Table 3.1 Percentage Forecasts of the 2008 President Election

Forecast	Nov. 2, noon Obama/McCain	Actual minus Forecast
Actual vote share	53.2/46.8	-
RCP Average of 11 Undecided allocated	53.6/46.4	-0.4
IEM vote share	53.0/47.0	+0.2
Fair forecast	51.9/48.1	+1.3
ABC News/ Washington Post	54.6/45.4	-1.4
Walker Market Model	51.4/48.6	+1.8

CHAPTER 4

ELECTION 2012 : OBAMA VS. ROMNEY[3]

INTRODUCTION

An elected official who is eligible for another term plans to concentrate on the programs he or she was elected to pursue and sometimes has to make morally difficult decisions. Much of a first term may be spent preparing and campaigning for a second term, after which he or she will not be subject to voters' approval. If the first-term office holder is not focused on re-election, the staff surely is.

Political scientists often recommend limiting a U.S. president to a single, six-year term, as Mexico allows. A one-term limit reduces an officeholder's accountability to the electorate unless egregious infractions warrant impeachment. The electorate should probably wonder, in some cases, why a first-term elected official is willing to pursue a "lame duck" second term.

Incumbency can be a benefit or a curse. Critics emphasize an incumbent's mistakes, missteps, and misstatements. Sometimes, the misstep was in elementary school! The incumbent's supporters will publicize every accomplishment, executive order, or piece of proposed legislation, regardless of whether it had any chance of being enacted.

If a private sector executive opposes an incumbent politician, the businessperson may appear to have no flaws, when, in fact, he or she has many flaws, but almost no public record. Senior public sector leaders and managers are under continual monitoring by the media and the public. That experience differs

---

[3] This chapter is developed from "The 2012 Presidential Election: Did Markets Matter?" published in THE JOURNAL OF ACCOUNTING & FINANCE in 2013. The author thanks the North American Business Press for their permission to use that material.

greatly from business decision-making behind a private-sector corporate shield.

For the 2012 presidential election, incumbent President Barack Obama opposed businessperson Mitt Romney. They each chose a vice presidential partner with considerable experience in Congress. Obama had established a strong relationship with his vice president, Joe Biden. Mitt Romney chose Paul Ryan, an experienced Congressman, as his running mate.

The Role of the Economy

Powell and Whitten (1993) studied political and economic factors for 102 elections in 19 industrialized countries from 1969 – 1988. They found that unemployment, inflation, or real GDP growth did not significantly impact political gains or losses for incumbent candidates. The impacts of these three economic variables are examined later in this Chapter. The time between gains or losses, by country and election, could explain the weak relationships that Powell and Whitten found. Fifty years ago, Stigler surveyed voters from both parties and found that high inflation substantially reduced an incumbent's chances for re-election.

Lewis-Beck convened a symposium (Lewis-Beck, 2009) to analyze the role of the economy and some unique factors on President Obama's 2008 election during the financial crisis. Lewis-Beck et al. (2013) and Campbell (2012, 2013) showed that the weak economy in 2012 deterred prospects for Obama's re-election but did not lead to his defeat.

Incumbency

Campbell (2013) captured some of the campaign environment when he called 2012 a "miserable election." An incumbent for whom the economy had been so weak in his first term is not likely to win re-election. However, the economy was improving in 2012, in contrast to 2008. Romney did not inspire enough voters for him, but he was more effective than Obama during their first debate. 2012 may have been one of the few presidential elections when the economy did not dominate incumbency because President Obama began his first term dealing with a dominant economic crisis. For 2008, unemployment was 7.3 percent, inflation was 3.8 percent, and real GDP growth was 1.3 percent.

Financial markets have increasingly impacted presidential elections since 1920. In addition, variations of measures of the economic variables in the Walker model are tested to see if economic growth and inflation measures strengthen the model's power. The statistical significance of the alternative measures does improve the ability to forecast. In addition, different measures to represent financial market volatility are contrasted in Table 4.2. A more sophisticated measure of the increasing importance of financial markets to the public is also tested in this Chapter.

CANDIDATES

Barack Obama

Much of Barack Obama's background and experience were delineated at the beginning of Chapter 3. He gained a great deal of confidence working as a community organizer. During his first term, he capitalized on his choices of an experienced vice president, cabinet, and team of White House Advisors. This was in contrast to President Jimmy Carter, elected in 1986, following Nixon's resignation, and appointed a staff with almost no Washington experience.

Obama is a Harvard Law *cum laude* graduate who served as President of the Harvard Law Review. After Harvard, he worked as a civil rights attorney for several years and served seven years as an Illinois state senator. He was elected to the U.S. Senate from Illinois and served four of his six-year term before winning the presidency. Working as a community organizer in South Chicago gave him an appreciation for the needs of impoverished families who believed they had little future and rare public support.

Although he was not actively involved in the U.S. financial industry, Obama learned from his banking and financial advisors that the costs of the 2008-2009 financial crisis would influence every program his Administration would hope to pursue.

Mitt Romney

The Romney family was not new to national politics. Mitt Romney's father, George Romney, had been an unsuccessful Republican candidate for president versus Richard Nixon in 1968. He accepted the cabinet position of Secretary of Housing and Urban Development in Nixon's Cabinet.

Mitt Romney developed a highly successful career with Bain and Company, a prominent business consulting firm in New England, and then became the Chief Executive Officer of Bain's investment subsidiary. Romney accepted the chair of the 2002 U.S. Olympiad in Salt Lake City when it was in a disastrous financial position and poorly managed. He rescued it with aggressive fundraising and improved management. President Bush and Mitt Romney opened the "games" on time and under budget in February 2002.

Romney leveraged his business success and public service to win the election for Governor in Massachusetts as the Republican candidate in November 2002. He was a rare species as a Republican Governor to be elected in the State of Massachusetts. He began an unsuccessful campaign to become the 2008 Republican presidential candidate to run against Obama.

As Governor, he was acclaimed for developing a successful state healthcare insurance program that opened in 2006. Much of that program became a pilot program for the ACA Obama proposed during his first year as President.

Romney had explored the Republican nomination for President in 2004. He realized he could not be a strong alternative to incumbent, conservative Republican George W. Bush. Bush vowed to deal severely with the Middle East and the 9/11 terrorists. John McCain opposed Bush for the 2004 nomination. As a Senator and Senate Foreign Relations Committee member, McCain understood the necessary planning to deal with Iraq. As a Vietnam War hero, McCain had an advantage in opposing Bush's re-nomination, and Romney decided not to enter the competition.

In 2007, Governor Romney continued to be appreciated for salvaging the February 2002 Utah Olympiad and developing the Massachusetts health insurance program. He announced he would pursue the 2008 Republican nomination for President. He had national name recognition, but by the beginning of 2008, it became clear that John McCain should be the Republican to challenge Barack Obama, who was unknown. Romney canceled his planned 2008 national campaign strategy and began organizing to win the 2012 Republican nomination.

Romney's Republican Nomination

Romney's 2012 campaign began a year in advance. Thirteen Republican candidates sought the nomination, but only four remained after the Iowa and New Hampshire primaries. The three opponents for Romney were Congressman Rick Santorum, former House Speaker Newt Gingrich, and Congressman Ron Paul. Romney won six states on Super Tuesday and did reasonably well in most early primaries. After Super Tuesday, his three active opponents suspended their campaigns and, at least to some degree, supported Romney. As former Massachusetts Governor, Romney was considered less conservative than his opponents and an establishment Republican candidate.

Romney's financial expertise made him an attractive candidate for 2012 as the economy continued to stagnate. Gross Domestic Product growth for 2011 and 2012 were 1.8 and 2.2 percent, respectively. Romney was touted for rejuvenating Bain and Company and then establishing Bain Capital. Romney's business success positioned him to lead the implementation of the Dodd-Frank legislation to strengthen the regulation of the banking and housing finance industries.

The Romneys were one of the leading families of the Mormon Church. Mitt was the first Mormon to become a nominee of a national political party. The Mormon Church is very private, and many Americans do not know much about it. This could have affected Mitt Romney's efforts to oppose Barack Obama in states where there was a strong conservative, evangelical presence.

Obama's Leadership

The Democrats controlled the House of Representatives and Senate leadership for Obama's first two years in office (2009-2011). His administration realized they might not have this level of support for long because mid-year elections rarely favor the White

House incumbent party. Obama determined his priorities and which programs could be enacted with modest Democratic majorities in each house of Congress.

His choice was to focus on enacting the Affordable Care Act (ACA) because it was unlikely to have any Republican support after 2011. ACA was enacted on March 23, 2010 and became known as Obamacare. The President, himself sometimes used this term. When Obamacare opened on October 1, 2013, it was a disaster. The website crashed on the first day and required months to reconfigure it. This contrast between Romney's state program and the national program did not escape the views of Obama's critics.

Obama was convinced from his work as a community organizer that ACA would be in the best long-run interests of the country. He recognized that without it, lower-income families might never obtain private health insurance, whose costs were rising by more than 10 percent yearly. The arguments against ACA were similar to those President Franklin Delano Roosevelt heard when he negotiated with Congress in the 1930s to enact Medicare and Medicaid. Fifty years after their enactment, they have become a primary financial support for many retirees and lower-income families.

A number of years later, the public learned that there was disagreement among Obama's senior staff about whether rebuilding the economy or enacting ACA should have been the top priority at the beginning of the Obama Administration. The President dictated that ACA would be the priority while the Democrats controlled each branch of Congress. He was more concerned with public policy needs than his prospects for re-election.

Early in his first presidential term, President Obama learned that issues other than those he campaigned on would require much of his attention. The continuing Middle East's hatred for the U.S. was clear. American voters continued to demand more protection from events like 9/11 and terrorism.

By the time of Obama's second inauguration, the rebuilding of lower Manhattan in New York and the Pentagon in Washington had begun. Families continued to mourn the 3,000 who died on

9/11. A large number of people who had worked in New York for years chose not to spend another day in the City, which caused many retail businesses to fail. Numerous large firms relocated from New York City to New Jersey, Connecticut, and New York suburbs like White Plains.

PARTICIPATION FINANCIAL MARKETS

The Financial Crisis

The beginning of the financial crisis was identified by the failure of Bear Stearns on March 15, 2008; as Obama was campaigning for the Democratic nomination, some party leaders were exploring a need for new, younger leadership. A few experts had spoken about the need for more attention to how housing finance and mortgages were being processed the year before. One person was Federal Reserve Board Governor Edward Gramlich. He recognized the danger of subprime lending (Gramlich, 2007) and disagreed with Federal Reserve Chairman Alan Greenspan and other governors, who thought Gramlich was overreacting to limited data.

Gramlich understood that banks and savings institutions were making loans at rates below market rates and selling the loans to Fannie Mae and Freddie Mac, which were supported with public funds. Fannie Mae and Freddie Mac raised funds at subsidized rates as government corporations with federal guarantees in fixed-income markets. The federal agencies incurred losses in the markets when they acquired the mortgages and incurred much greater losses when the borrowers defaulted. The private lenders were not maintaining reasonable lending standards or requiring proper collateral for their loans since the institutions knew they would sell the loans and did not even attempt to collect them.

By 2010, U.S. financial markets began to return to some normality after numerous institutions failed in 2008 and 2009. This followed a 32.5 percent one-year stock market crash between October 2007 and October 2008. (See Table 4.1). After the 2008 election, the stock market began a slow, gradual recovery long before the government's efforts to stimulate the economy had much effect.

It was not until 2012 that the Dow Jones Index reached its October 2007 level. From October 30, 2009 to October 30, 2012, the Dow Jones Industrial Average increased an average of 9.9 percent per year to reach 13,107 in October. This was still 760 points below its October 2007 level. (See Table 4.1). Annual per capita Gross Domestic Product Growth was -0.3 percent in 2008 and -2.5 percent in 2009.

President Obama re-nominated Dr. Ben Bernanke to be Chairman of the Board of Governors of the Federal Reserve in February 2012. His Ph.D. dissertation focused on the Depression of the 1930s. After the October 2008 financial market crash, Bernanke commented that his research had prepared him uniquely to understand the crisis and recession. Bernanke was one of the financial experts who brought the economy out of the recession.

The recession lasted eight quarters, from the fourth quarter of 2007 through the third quarter of 2009. The National Bureau of Economic Research (NBER) has been entrusted since the 1940s to identify recessions in the U.S. economy. According to the NBER, "a recession is the period between a peak of economic activity and its subsequent trough, or lowest point. Between trough and peak, the economy is in an expansion." (NBER, 2024) The NBER's definition emphasizes that a recession involves a significant decline in economic activity spread across the economy and lasting more than a few months.

This 8-quarter recession is a testament to the work of the financial regulators. Congress enacted the TARP (Troubled Asset Relief Program) program on September 30, 2008 (Gaby and Walker, 2011). TARP had the impossible provision that regulators should evaluate the toxic assets of all the undercapitalized banks and savings institutions. This could have required hundreds of staff working several years.

The regulators developed an alternative in which undercapitalized large and medium-sized banks and savings institutions sold preferred stock to the U.S. Treasury. The stock had a five percent annual dividend to be paid to the Treasury with a five-year lifetime. At the end of five years, the institution must either buy back the preferred stock from the Treasury or increase the dividend to nine percent. Some institutions complained they would not be capable of repurchasing the stock within five years (by 2013) and that a nine percent dividend would bankrupt them. They argued that they would have to seek a partner to acquire them. The regulators had no sympathy and explained that five years and five percent were generous terms. The regulators argued that five years was a generous period for an institution to reorganize its balance sheet, and a five percent dividend was low under the circumstances.

Financial Markets' Extensions to the Model

To forecast the 2012 election, the Walker Model is extended to include increasing annual financial markets' activity and the impact of the financial crisis. Fair's database began with the 1920 presidential election, where T = 0. To forecast the popular vote in Chapter 3, a simple financial variable was added to the model, T = 22. The variable that was created for 2008 was the annual Dow Jones (DJ) percentage growth, weighted by a time trend T, T = 0, 1, 2, ...,22.

$$Z(T) = \% \, \Delta DJ * T. \tag{4.1}$$

The Walker popular vote forecast for 2008 had the largest error, 1.8 percent, among the five comparable systems in Table 3.1.

For the 2012 election, a more sophisticated financial term is introduced into the model to include increasing interest and participation in financial markets over time (T0 = 0 < t < 22).

The term is

$$W(T) = \{\% \, \Delta \, DJ\} \, e^{\, r(t-T0)} \tag{4.2}$$

After the stock market crash, regulators and creative bankers developed new financial instruments to motivate consumers to increase their savings. Institutions required larger down payments to obtain a mortgage and considerably more proof that the borrower could make the payments. A larger segment of the population began to increase their savings for retirement and children's and grandchildren's 529 college plans, IRA savings accounts, new retirement plans, and money market mutual funds. Financial advisors became aware that social security and modest employer pensions would not enable clients to retire comfortably.

T0 = 0 in equation (4.2) and T = 23 to predict the 2012 election popular vote. r is the growth rate of the country's interest in financial markets. The estimated value for r is 0.15, and the second component of equation (4.2) is e $^{0.15\,T}$.

Model 4D in Table 4.2 contrasts the measures of financial market impacts in Chapters 3 and 4. The W coefficient in model 4D is 1.91 with a t-statistic of 2.25, which is statistically significantly different from zero at the five percent probability level.

Table 4.2 provides two previously applied models, where different financial terms are tested as extensions to the Walker Model. Model 4D captures Individuals' and investors' increasing interest in financial markets. Among the four models, 4A – 4D, for any particular variable, the coefficients and t-statistics are similar. For inflation, for example, the coefficients range from -0.24 to -0.33, and the t-statistics range from -2.24 to -2.72. The coefficients are all statistically significantly different from zero at the five percent probability level.

The adjusted R^2 values range from 0.67 to 0.75, and the F-statistics range from 7.04 to 9.86. These test statistics are relatively low compared to models for earlier elections.

The Walker financial model (4D in Table 4.2) forecasts the 2012 popular vote for Obama. V_{2012} is predicted to be 51.1 percent, Obama's share of the popular vote. For 2012, Table 4.3 shows that many of the 2012 forecasts were quite close. However, shortly before Election Day, several forecasts predicted that Romney would receive more than 50 percent of the 2012 popular vote. One Gallup poll conducted two days before the election predicted the candidates would be tied. Obama received 332 Electoral Votes, and Romney received 206.

WAR, GROWTH, ANG INFLATION

The relatively large error in predicting the popular vote for 2008 with the Walker Model encouraged testing a variety of different measures to represent War, Growth, and Inflation for the 2012 forecast.

War

Excluding Korea and Vietnam as war election years to predict the presidential popular vote was shown to be too narrow an assumption in Chapter 2. The increased statistical significance of the coefficient of WAR between the Fair and Walker models (equations F and W, respectively) is the evidence. The number of troops called for duty, and the ugly battles with terrorists in Iraq recommend that 2004 and 2008 be coded as War election years.

Three alternatives for measuring WAR have been tested to examine the effects of different war election years.
- WAR1 = 1 for 1920, 1944, 1948, 1952, 1968, 1972, 2004, 2008 and 0 otherwise.
- WAR2 = 1 for 1944, 1952, 1968, 1972 and 0 otherwise.
- WAR3 = 1 for 1944, 1952, 1968, 1972, 2004, 2008 and 0 otherwise.

WAR1 is the measure that has been included as Wartime elections in the four models in Table 4.2.

The coefficients of WAR range from 2.22 to 2.35 and are all statistically significantly different from zero at the five percent probability level. In Chapter One, the t-statistics for the coefficient of WAR in Fair's model are significant at only the 20 percent probably level.

The war histories beyond Fair's original coding were one of Walker's three initial extensions to Fair's fundamental model (F). The Biden Administration's limited support for Afghanistan and vigorous support for Israel for 2024, although there are no "boots on the ground," will be somewhat controversial as to whether 2024 should be considered a war election year. The U.S. economy is stimulated when wartime goods and equipment are supplied to our Allies. Whether that makes 2024 a war election year is discussed in Chapter 7.

Growth

Economic growth is a determinant of the popular vote, although it is often highly correlated with other economic measures. Fair argues that the effect of economic growth is not so great until the first three quarters of the election year, particularly in the second and third quarters (see Table 4.1). Fair observed that economic growth the year **before** the presidential election does not substantially influence voters' decisions on Election Day.

Real Gross Domestic Product (GDP) growth of approximately 2.5 percent is necessary to create new jobs in an economy. A growth rate of 2.0 does not create many new jobs. For President Obama's campaign for a second term, the per capita GDP growth rates were 2.6 percent for 2010 and 2.2 percent for 2012. Obama's policies are credited with saving the auto industry with large quantities of federal government purchases of new vehicles during the recession.

Economic growth measures have been tested for the models in Table 4.2. The growth measures are time-weighted real per capita GDP (GDP/POPULATION) variations for election year T and quarter j, j = 1,2,3.

(1) Declining weighted average of election year first and second quarters
$$G1 = (2/3) (GDP/POP)_{T,2} + (1/3) (GDP/POP)_{T,1}$$

(2) Average election year first and second quarters
$$G2 = (1/2) (GDP/POP)_{T,2} + (1/2) (GDP/POP)_{T,1}$$

(3) Average election year three quarters
$$G3 = (1/3) (GDP/POP)_{T,3} + (1/3) (GDP/POP)_{T,2} + (1/3) (GDP/POP)_{T,1}$$

G1 has a statistically significant coefficient at the one percent probability level. The smallest correlation among these growth measures is 0.85.

Inflation

Recall that Stigler (1973) surveyed the importance of inflation on voters' choices 50 years ago. His results influenced Fair to include INFLATION in his models. High inflation shortly before a presidential election makes it difficult for an incumbent to be re-elected. Federal Reserve Open Market Committee (FOMC) Members' statements, the Chair's statement after each FOMC meeting, and statements by other FOMC members concerning current and future inflation and growth have a measurable effect on financial markets. Many investors and "Fed Watchers" pay great attention to these statements.

For 2011 – 2012 and 2012-2013, the year-over-year inflation rates were 1.4 percent and 2.0 percent, respectively. Voters should have been quite satisfied with those rates after the difficult decade that preceded the 2012 election.

Three inflation measures are tested for the models in Table 4.2. The measures are constructed analogously to the growth measures.

(1) Declining weighted average of election year first and second quarters
$$INF1 = (2/3) (INF)_{T,2} + (1/3) (INF)_{T,1}$$

(2) Average election year first and second quarters
$$INF2 = (1/2) (INF)_{T,2} + (1/2) (INF)_{T,1}$$

(3) Average election year three quarters
$$INF3 = (1/3) (INF)_{T,3} + (1/3) (INF)_{T,2} + (1/3) (INF)_{T,1}$$

Measure (1) is the one employed in the models in Table 4.2.

CONCLUSIONS

The 2012 presidential opponents were a successful businessperson, who was the first Mormon on a major party ticket, and the first African-American incumbent president in the nation's history. Neither man had a career as a politician.

During the 2012 presidential election year, GDP growth rates for the first three quarters were 2.0, 1.3, and 2.7 percent, respectively. Inflation was no larger than 2.0 percent. Preliminary data for the fourth quarter were not available until spring 2013.

These data are collected and reported by the U.S. Bureau of Economic Analysis. They are carefully protected from political influence from either party.

With the data that were available the first week in November, 2012, it would have been difficult to unseat an incumbent. This subject is a major issue discussed in chapters 6 and 7.

TABLE 4.1 ECONOMIC AND STOCK MARKET DATA

Year	ANNUAL GDP GROWTH	INFLATION year-over year percentage change	DJ 10/31	DJ*** year-over-year percentage change
2007	1.9%		13,870	
		+5.6%		-32.5%
2008	-0.3%		9,325	
		-2.1%		+5.8%
2009	-2.5%		9,868	
		+1.2%		+12.7%
2010	2.6%		11,125	
		+3.6%		+7.7%
2011	1.5%		11,983	
		+1.4%		+9.4%
2012	2.2%		13,107	
		+2.0%		+18.8%
2013	1.8%		15,569	

*** 2009-2010-2011-2012 average of 3 percentage changes = 9.9%

TABLE 4.2 ECONOMICS AND MARKET MODELS 1920 – 2008

(t-statistics in parentheses)
(t-statistics above 2.07 are statistically significant at the 5% level)

	MODEL 4A	MODEL 4B	MODEL 4C	MODEL 4D
CONSTANT	46.28 (31.28))	46.43 (32.66)	48.26 (30.58	46.55 (35.54)
GROWTH	0.62 (4.65)	0.62 (4.79)	0.62 (4.54)	0.61 (5.16)
INFLATION	-0.30 (-2.47)	-0.32 (-2.72)	-0.33 (-2.52)	-0.24 (-2.24)
GOODNEWS	0.96 (4.44)	0.88 (4.08)	0.94 (4.24)	0.84 (4.24)
%Δ DJ		0.11 (1.65)		
% ΔDJ * T			0.01 (0.73)	
%ΔDJ $^{e0.15t}$				1.91 (2.25)
PARTY	-1.84 (-2.54)	-1.82 (-2.63)	-1.88 (-2.54)	-1.64 (-2.56)
WAR	3.32 (2.28)	3.12 (2.22)	3.34 (2.24)	3.03 (2.35)
AR(1)	-0.73 (-4.11)	-0.70 (-3.63)	-0.71 (-3.78)	-0.74 (-4.17)
$\bar{R}^2$	0.68	0.71	0.67	0.75
F	8.38	8.39	7.04	9.86
DW	2.38	2.27	2.36	2.31

TABLE 4.3 ELECTION 2012 FORECAST

Source	Incumbent Share	Obama Minus Source = Error	Date in 2012	Source
Obama Vote Romney Vote Others Vote	51.1% 47.2% 1.7%	-	2021	*The President's Fact Book*
Walker Market Model	51.1%	0	10/31	"The 2012 U.S. Presidential Election" J. of Acctg. & Finance
Fair	51.6%	0.5%	10/26	http://fairmodel.econ.yale. Yale.edu/vote2012/index2
IEM	50.6%	0.5 %	11/5	www.iemweb.biz.uiowa. edu/PriceHistory
NBC/WSJ	50.5%	0.6 %	11/4	http://firstread.nbcnews. com/news/2012/11/01
CNN	50.0%	1.1 %	11/4	www.cnn.com/POLITICS/ pollingcenter/index
Many Others	Obama below 50 %		between 10/23 & 11/5	

Definition of Walker's Variables

VOTE = the incumbent share of the two-party presidential vote.

GR = per capita election year GDP growth rate in quarters 1-3 .

INFL = absolute value of growth rate of GDP deflator in the first 15 quarters of the administration.

GDNES = quarters of the first 15 quarters of an administration when real per capita GDP growth > 3.2 annual %.

PERSON = 1 if the incumbent is running for re-election, and 0 otherwise.

DUR = 0 if the incumbent party is in power for 1 term, 1 if the incumbent is in power for 2 consecutive terms, 1.25 if incumbent is in power for 3 consecutive terms.

PARTY= 1 if there is a Democratic incumbent at the time of the election and -1 if there is a Republican incumbent.

WAR = 1 for 1920, 1944, 1948, 1952, 1968, and 1972.

CHAPTER 5

NEOPHITE TRUMP VS. CLINTON[4]

INTRODUCTION

In 2016, for the second time in the current century, the presidential candidate who won the U.S. popular vote was not elected President. Donald Trump received 306 Electoral Votes, although Hillary Rodham Clinton received 51.1 percent of the popular vote. The winner of the Electoral College vote did not win the popular vote in four other American presidential elections: 1824, 1876, 1888, and 2000. Matuz (2009, p.30) summarizes the "The Electoral College Through the ears."

In Federalist Paper No. 68, Alexander Hamilton (1788) recommended that the Electoral College winner should become president. Hamilton argued that the Electoral College allows the appropriate involvement by the public to elect the President. He claimed that the Electoral College requires the public to be represented by well-informed, politically competent electors who should make the selection on behalf of the population, some of whom may not be able or trusted to make a choice. Hamilton defended the Electoral College system to be a check on potential corruption or chaos in the process.

The Walker popular vote model (W), developed in Chapter 2, is applied in this Chapter to forecast the 2016 popular vote. Recall the foundation is the original Fair model (F) with the enhancements. A probit model was developed following the 2016 election to examine how Trump won the Electoral College.

---

[4] This chapter is developed from "How They Lost The Presidency" published in APPLIED ECONOMICS in March 2018. The author thanks Taylor & Francis for their permission to use that material.

THE 2016 CANDIDATES

DONALD J. TRUMP

Donald J. Trump was elected as the 45th President in November 2016 with 306 Electoral Votes, defeating Hillary Rodham Clinton, who won the popular vote. Trump is the only president who never served in the military nor in public office (*Washington Post*, 2016b).

Trump was a well-known New York real estate tycoon who was regarded as a difficult businessperson. Many employees left Trump's employment, especially in Atlantic City, New Jersey, claiming they were owed wages and benefits. They did not have the resources to pursue their claims through the legal system.

Trump's business "success" has a tarnished record. His failed businesses included Trump Airlines, Trump University, the Tahj Mahal Casino, and several other Atlantic City, New Jersey casinos that carried Trump's name.

Trump's business successes were often a result of applying high proportions of debt and leverage. His depreciation and interest expenses often minimized his tax obligations and took advantage of other provisions in the U.S. tax code. On May 31, 2024, a jury of 12 persons residing in New York convicted Trump of all 34 charges of illegal business practices.

Politician

Trump has been a member of three political parties. First, he joined the Reform Party (1987-1999), after which he became a Democrat (2001-2009). He switched to the Republican Party in 2010. He was probably first known in the political world when he challenged Barack Obama's eligibility to be a presidential candidate. The challenge was known as the "birther "issue. In 2011, Trump claimed that Obama was not born in the United States and that he should be prohibited from serving as president. Trump was considering becoming a presidential candidate in 2012 to oppose Obama's re-election Eventually, Obama released the long form of his birth certificate proving he was born in the State of

Hawaii and that his parents were an American mother and Kenyan father.

Donald Trump's 2016 presidential campaign insulted virtually every respectable candidate and many distinguished persons. He called his Republican opponents by uncomplimentary nicknames. During the primaries and until he was the presumed Republican nominee, he insulted virtually all of his Republican opponents with comments about their physical appearance or their family members' appearance. He lied about some of their personal behavior (much of which he was personally guilty). He mainly appealed to supporters who were not mainstream political participants.

This behavior continued from when he developed and performed on his cable television shows - The Apprentice and Celebrity Apprentice. When he informed a rejected candidate that he or she was not selected to work for him permanently, Trump screamed at the person, "YOU'RE FIRED." This was part of Trump's intended humor, but candidates rarely "enjoyed" the humor.

During one presidential debate, the Trump Campaign Organization attempted to seat several women directly in front of Mrs. Clinton's lectern. These women were rumored to have had affairs with the candidate's husband.

During a one-on-one debate with Secretary Clinton after the parties nominating conventions, Trump left his platform, walked behind her, nearly touched her, and berated her while she was answering a question from the moderator. In almost every campaign debate, Trump violated rules that had been agreed upon by his campaign representatives. Sometimes, he insulted moderators. More stringent rules have been agreed upon for the 2024 debates.

One important component of the Trump campaign to win the nomination and then to pursue the presidency was strong, positive support from Russia. Foreign election interference is improper and illegal according to the U.S. Constitution. The Trump Campaign was exposed for a meeting at Trump Towers between senior Russian officials offering to support the Trump campaign and Trump's representatives. Trump was represented by his son,

Donald Jr.; his son-in-law, Jerad Kushner; and Trump campaign manager, Paul Manafort (later sentenced to prison for other criminal activity). Russians hacked into the Democratic National Committee's database and used the data to humiliate Democratic candidate Clinton and falsely accuse her of crimes in which she claimed she had no involvement, and no proof was ever suggested. Senior Russian leaders had a contentious relationship with Mrs. Clinton when she was First Lady and again when she was Secretary of State.

After Trump was inaugurated, he appointed Robert S. Muller to investigate claims about Trump's Russian connections and support. Muller had been the sixth director of the Federal Bureau of Investigation and was endorsed by four presidents. Mr. Mueller is a distinguished Republican who served in several top government positions. Mueller concluded that the Russian violations and evidence were improper for a presidential candidate. Meuller decided, however, that the evidence was not sufficient to indict **and** convict a sitting president, unless there was also a Congressional investigation and impeachment. Mr. Mueller clearly stated that he did not disagree with the charges he was investigating.

Trump's Abusive Behavior Toward Immigrants

Throughout the 2016 campaign and the debates, Trump made ugly, offensive comments about almost every minority and immigrant group in America. He claimed that immigrants were taking over the country and "they should go back to where they came from." One of his campaign promises was that he would build a wall on the border between the U.S. and Mexico to retrain potential immigrants from Mexico, Central America, and South America, and he would force Mexico to pay for the wall.

A modest, ineffective wall was constructed mostly with funds authorized for other programs. Mexico did not contribute anything toward the construction. Many foreigners continued to enter the U.S. illegally through Mexico. To deal with the issue, the Trump Administration implemented a shameful public policy of separating young children from their parents when they were arrested in the U.S. and made no effort to reunite the families. The Biden

Administration spent a fortune and years trying to reconnect children with their parents.

Trump Economics

Trump believed there were two major difficulties with the U.S. economy. First, he advocated and signed legislation to reduce taxes, especially corporate taxes, to stimulate employment and economic growth. Personal taxes on high-income taxpayers were reduced, which endeared them to Trump. The fiscal deficit increased considerably during the Trump Administration. Much of the increase resulted from the federal government's lower tax revenues.

Second, Trump was convinced that our foreign trading partners were taking advantage of the U.S. because of our historically unfavorable trade balance (exports < imports) with the rest of the world, especially China. This was one of Trump's campaign pronouncements that he continued through his four years as President. U.S. businesses produced considerably more goods than the world bought than our imports.

HILLARY RODHAM CLINTON

Hillary Rodham Clinton has an extensive political history. (Her first name is used in places in this text to distinguish her from her husband and not to denigrate her in any disrespectful manner.) She served in more political positions than almost any other person did in U.S. history. She was born and raised in the Chicago area, which has its own political connotations thanks to Mayor Richard J. Daley (mayor until December 1976). Many claim Mayor Daley made John F. Kennedy President in 1960 (because of Illinois' irregular vote "counting") and Richard M. Nixon president in 1968 (because of the manner in which Chicago police "handled protestors" and massive riots during the 1968 Chicago Democratic convention).

Secretary Clinton began her political activity as a teenager, volunteering for conservative Republican candidate Senator Barry Goldwater, who lost to incumbent Democrat Lyndon Baines Johnson in the 1964 landside. While she was a student at Wellesley, she worked at the 1968 Miami Republican convention that nominated Richard Nixon. Afterward, she became a liberal Rockefeller Republican.

Hillary Clinton became a liberal Democrat near the time she graduated from Wellesley. For law school, she chose Yale, where she met Bill Clinton, whom she dated. He proposed marriage to her upon graduation, as he continually did until she finally accepted. They were married in 1975, a year after they moved to Arkansas.

Hillary Clinton's Breadth of Experiences

Early in her legal career, Hillary Clinton accepted a range of opportunities to gain political insights beyond her experience. In 1972, she and her future husband campaigned for George McGovern in Texas, where it was obvious he had no chance to win. In 1974, she worked as a staff member for the Watergate Congressional Committee, which developed critical material to support Nixon's Impeachment. That summer, DC Judge John Sirica required Nixon to turn over his office recordings and tapes that proved Nixon's active involvement in the Republican burglary of the Democratic Watergate Headquarters in Washington. In 1976, Mrs. Clinton took a leave of absence from her law practice in Arkansas to gain experience as the campaign director for Democratic candidate Jimmy Carter in Indiana.

Arkansas

After law school, Bill Clinton returned to Arkansas to pursue legal and political careers. Hillary Rodham followed him, and they both taught at the University of Arkansas Law School. Two years later, she joined The Rose Law firm, a prestigious Arkansas firm with major political connections throughout the state.

Hillary Rodham Clinton developed her political and professional career with her husband, as they said on a "60 Minutes" CBS interview. They said if Bill Clinton were elected president in 1992, the country would get "Two for the Price of One." Mrs. Clinton's presidential candidacy followed an active political career that included:

1974: moved to Arkansas with Bill as he lost a Congressional election

1975: married Bill Clinton in October

1976: supported Bill's successful campaign for Arkansas Attorney General

1977: joined The Rose Law Firm

1978: supported Bill's successful campaign to be elected Governor of Arkansas

1978 –1992: Arkansas First Lady and employed by the Arkansas Legal Services Board of Directors;1978-1979 successfully trading cattle futures

1980: daughter Chelsea born. Bill lost re-election for governor

1982 – 1992: Bill continually re-elected governor, the First Lady Joined several boards of directors, TCBY, Wall Mart, etc.

1991: Bill & Hillary began campaign for the White House. Little Democratic competition to run against the incumbent; George H. W. Bush had won the war in the Gulf; having 80% national popularity in January

1992: fall: U.S. economy in shambles, Pres. Bush seemed out of touch, stumbling while walking at Camp David, and fell asleep at prime minister's Japanese state dinner on his behalf

1993 - 2001: active First Lady; Bill Clinton impeached by the House

2000: a Senate seat from N.Y. and serving as First Lady; expected to oppose Rudy Giuliani, who withdrew for health reasons

2001 - 2006: Hillary elected and serving as U.S. Senator from New York

2006: re-elected Senator from New York

2008: opposed Obama for Democratic nomination for president, winning more elected delegates, but winning few Super Delegates

2009 – 2012: U.S. Secretary of State; Libya mission attacked, Bengazi fiasco where U.S. Ambassador was killed

2013 - 2014: organizing campaign to run for President for 2016

2015 - 2016: campaigned for the Democratic nomination for
President
2016: Democrats presidential candidate

After she had won the Democratic nomination for president, Mrs. Clinton gave a series of private lectures to senior executives of Goldman Sachs investment bank charging substantial fees. Republicans charged this was illegal, or at least inappropriate, campaign fundraising. Mrs. Clinton claimed the fees were earned for the Clinton Foundation and had nothing to do with her campaign.

Mrs. Clinton probably accepted more responsibility than any First Lady in history. She led the Administration's 1993-1995 failed effort to enact the first national health insurance program. The failure was partly because of her political naiveté dealing with Congress. She created children's programs that the Administration implemented. The First Lady became involved in the politics of staffing the Administration's travel office, which was labeled the Travelgate fiasco.

Mrs. Clinton was criticized for how she handled confidential and secret emails on her private server while she served as Secretary of State. She was accused of transferring secret and confidential information through her personal email system rather than using the secure State Department System. Mrs. Clinton did not deny the criticism, but she replied that this resulted from her incompetence with complicated technology, which was true for most of her generation.

POPULAR VOTE MODELS

Fundamental Popular Vote Model

For 2016, the unique term that was introduced into the Walker popular vote model was a measure of the level of competition among candidates pursuing the nomination for the *out-of-power party*. The competition is denoted by CANDID, measured by the number of candidates nominated at that party's national convention. This variable represents the number of primary opponents who challenged Trump. Initially, there were eleven competitors in the primaries. This was the most competitive primary process since the Democratic race in 1972. Trump was underestimated as a candidate mainly because he lacked political experience and had an unusual style.

Estimated Popular Vote Model

The Walker Popular Vote Model for 2016 is estimated from Fair's election-year database from 1900 through 2012. This is a longer time series than was previously available to estimate models developed by Fair or Walker.

The dependent variable, V_{2016}, is the share of the two-party popular vote received by the Democratic Party's candidate since Democrats were the White House incumbent party. The variables tested in previous studies by Walker and Fair are inflation, real GDP growth, the length of time an incumbent party has been in office (Duration), candidate incumbency, and whether the election occurred during a war year. Numbers in parentheses () below each coefficient are t-statistics for the coefficient.

$$V= 53.27 - 0.82 \, INFL + 7.40 \, INCUM - 0.38 \, CANDID - 6.16 \, DUR + 4.50 \, WAR + 0.34 \, GR - 0.43 \, AR(1) \quad (5.1)$$
$$\quad (31.51) \; (-4.02) \quad (5.01) \qquad (-2.64) \qquad (-3.67) \quad (1.93) \quad (2.01) \quad (-1.78)$$

CANDID, the new variable for the 2016 model, ranged from peaks of 21 in 1916 and 20 in 1972 to a low of 1 in 1900 and 2 in four other elections. The median is eight. Nine candidates were nominated at the 2016 Republican Convention, making that convention more competitive than any since 1972.

Table 5.1 presents adjusted R-squares and t-statistics for the coefficients of alternative models to predict the percentage of the two-party popular vote for the Democrats. The model that appears in the first row is selected because its coefficients are consistently statistically significant. The adjusted R-square is 0.54. The column denoted AR(1)/DW reports the t-statistic for the coefficient of AR(1) if the Durbin-Watson (DW) statistic indicates the AR transformation is needed to remove auto-correlation.

The Durbin-Watson statistic indicates whether the error terms between successive elections are correlated or not so much. The DW ranges between 0 and 4.0. A DW near 2.0 indicates that the errors are not highly correlated. A DW close to 0 or 4 indicates the errors are negatively or positively correlated, respectfully.

With an AR(1) transformation, Durbin-Watson statistics become closer to 2.0. The DW in the far right column is reported alone if the adjustment for autocorrelation is not necessary.

The Democratic candidate's popular vote percentage varies inversely with inflation and positively with economic growth. The longer Democrats occupied the White House, the smaller the Democratic share of the popular vote is expected to be. The expected Democratic vote share decreases if there has been a Democratic President for a number of terms. If a Democratic incumbent is running, the expected Democratic share of the two-party popular vote increases since the coefficient of Incumbent is positive and statistically significant.

The coefficient of WAR has a positive sign. If there were a war during an election year, the Democratic nominee is expected to win.

If the out-of-power party has a highly competitive presidential nomination, the Democratic vote share is expected to be lower, indicated by the negative sign of the coefficient for CANDID. The contentious Republican nominating process seems to have increased voters' interest in Republican Donald Trump since he was new to politics and campaigned in an unconventional manner.

Among the additional variables that have been tested, none has a statistically significant coefficient different from 0 at the 5 percent probability level. These variables include unemployment, third-party candidates, the year-end Dow Jones Average, candidates' political experience, and an economic policy index.

An economic policy index has not been tested in this context because of potential conflicts among the index's components t. The index has a correlation coefficient of 0.55 with the year-end Dow Jones Average. Its potential election impact was tested implicitly in earlier chapters.

The selected model to predict the 2016 popular vote is from line 1 of Table 5.1 and Equation 5.1. The alternative models have at least one coefficient of a major variable in the primary model with a low t-statistic. Introducing variables beyond the selected model reduces the t-statistics for either Growth, War, or both coefficients. Both variables are important for voters when choosing between candidates, as has been found in other studies to determine the presidential popular vote.

Popular Vote Forecast

Table 5.2 provides forecasts of Secretary Clinton's 2016 popular vote based on the selected model on the first line of Table 5.1. Median values of the independent variables are given in the body of Table 5.2. The medians are substituted for independent variables into the enhanced model (W) to obtain the forecast. Medians are preferred to avoid the effects of skewed measures of some variables.

Mrs. Clinton's popular vote forecast is 50.5 percent, based on the medians for six previous elections (1992-2012). A revised forecast is 51.8 percent, based on the medians for a shorter, more recent period, 2000-2012 (only four elections). These forecasts were published Monday, November 7, the day before the 2016 election, along with a forecast based on measures of independent variables for only the first three quarters of 2016 (https://finpolicy.georgetown.edu/).

The average of the two forecasts (50.5 and 51.8) is that Secretary Clinton would receive 51.1 percent of the two-party popular vote from the 50 states and the District of Columbia. This forecast compares favorably with the major national pollsters' final 2016 presidential election surveys.

ELECTORAL COLLEGE MODEL AND VOTE

Trump was acknowledged as the winner of the presidency on election night of 2016. A probit model was developed for this election (with a binary dependent variable) subsequent to the November 8, 2016 election. This model was not employed to predict the 2016 Electoral College vote since it was developed after the election. Its purpose was to explain, *ex-ante,* the difference in the results of the popular and electoral vote winners.

The 2016 Electoral College Model is a 50-state, cross-section probit model to explain Trump's Electoral College victory. The dependent variable is 1.0 if Trump won a state's popular vote and

0.0 otherwise. The estimated model is Equation (5.2). Estimated probit coefficients have a z distribution (analogous to the t-distribution with many observations). The numbers under the coefficients in brackets [ ] are z-score statistics.

REP 2016 ST = 44.54 – .0016 ST per capita - 1.5005 %Δ ST + .0815 % ST REP
State win = 1   [2.83]   [-2.60]   income   [-2.05] GDP   [2.09]   senators
State loss = 0

       -.3246 % Hispanic ST population   + .0003 ST population   (5.2)
       [-2.49]   [2.87]

The cross-section Electoral College Model includes statewide variables analogous to the Popular Vote Model variables. The potential factorsinclude states' economic conditions (per capita income and percentage changes in state GDP), political environment (numbers of Republican state senators in the legislature), population size, educational levels, and gender and racial populations.

2016 Electoral College Model (Table 5.3)

Table 5.3 provides z-statistics for the 2016 election probit cross-section models after applying a White robust heteroskedastic transformation. The model on the first line is the best explanation, *ex-ante*, of significant factors for Trump's Electoral College victory. This model has the highest adjusted R-square (0.87), nearly the lowest AKAIKE IC value (0.42), and five statistically significant coefficients at the five percent probability level or better. These test statistics support selecting the first line in Table 5.3 as the model to predict Trump's Electoral College victory. In cases where the adjusted R-square is nearly as high, the coefficient of at least one important explanatory variable does not have a significant z-statistic at a meaningful probability.

The negative coefficients of variables representing a state's economy — per-capita income and real GDP growth — indicate that states with weaker economies were more likely to vote for Trump. The states with a higher percentage of Republicans in the U.S. Senate (SENREPUB) also voted for Trump. The positive sign for the coefficient of population (POP) reflects Trump's victories in more populous states. The political party of a state's governor had a less significant coefficient than a state's representation in the U.S. Senate. Trump won the U.S. presidency by winning some of the largest states (Pennsylvania, Michigan, and Wisconsin with 45 electoral votes) by small vote margins and states with low per capita incomes and weak economic growth. Trump also lost the minority vote by less than was expected.

Other independent variables were introduced into the primary model to test for additional potential explanations for Trump's victory. State unemployment (U) was included in several models. All coefficients of U had low z-statistics, and these models exhibited higher AKAIKE IC values, well above the lowest one. Economic growth and income have statistically more important coefficients than unemployment in explaining whether a state voted for Trump.

States with lower percentages of Hispanic populations were more likely to vote for Trump, as indicated by this coefficient's negative and statistically significant z-statistic. The mixed z-statistic signs for the percentage of the state population that is African American (AFRAMER) indicate that states with higher percentages of African Americans did not consistently vote for Secretary Clinton, as expected.

These results are consistent with the reported changes in the size of the Hispanic and African American voter turnout in 2016. The state minority population is also tested as the **sum** of the percentages of Hispanic and African American populations. This is indicated in Table 5.3 by repeating the same z-statistic in columns labeled HISPANIC and AFRAMER. The models have somewhat lower adjusted R-squared and higher AKAIKE IC values.

To represent a state's political persuasion at the time of the 2016 election, three other variables were tested: the number of the state's U.S. Senators who were Republicans (SENREP), the number of the state's U.S. House members who were Republicans, and whether the state has a Republican Governor (GOVREP). Among SENREP, HOUSREP, and GOVREP, the coefficient of SENREP has the greatest statistical significance.

Some analysts claim that less educated people voted for Donald Trump. Each education variable has a negative coefficient, indicating that less education in a state was consistent with

Trump's Electoral College victory. A state was less likely to vote for Trump if it had a larger percentage of people with a high school diploma (HSGRAD) or a bachelor's degree (BACH). The coefficient for greater high school graduation rates is statistically significant at only the 10 percent probability level, but in that model, the significance of the coefficient of GDP growth declines to 10 percent, the AKAIKE IC rises to 0.52, and the adjusted R-square declines to 0.79.

The percentages of a state's senior citizens or women population were tested as potential electoral vote determinants. Neither of these characteristics has a statistically significant coefficient at any meaningful level; each coefficient has a z-statistic below 1.0. Secretary Clinton was surely expected to win the electoral votes in states where women were a larger portion of the voting population. It was reported that more than 50 percent of white women voted for President Trump (CNN, 2016).

CONCLUSIONS

The day **before** the 2016 election, this Chapter was released to forecast the 2016 U.S. presidential election popular vote. The model is similar to the ones the author developed, based on the foundation of Fair's models. The 2016 model includes an additional variable representing the competitive environment for the out-of-power party competition, CANDID, in selecting its nominee. The statistical results are strong, and the popular vote forecast of 51.1 percent for Secretary Clinton is closer to the actual outcome than virtually every poll conducted immediately before the election.

Ex-ante, the author developed a 50-state, cross-section probit model to *understand* the 2016 Electoral College outcome and the difference between it and the popular vote result. Statistically, the probit model is strong. The five independent variables have absolute values of their z statistics between 2.05 and 2.87

TABLE 5. 1. POPULAR VOTE REGRESSION MODELS 1900 – 2016

t-statistics for coefficients of variables included in the model

adj. R square	INFLATION	GROWTH	DURATION	INCUMBENT	CANDID	WAR	AR(1)/DW #	ADDITIONAL VARIABLES
0.54	-4.02	2.01	-3.67	5.01	-2.64	1.93	-1.78	
0.54	-4.23	2.12	-3.95	5.36	-2.84	2.25	-2.09	'-1.12 dow at year end
0.58	-4.73	2.65	-3.44	5.19	-2.41	0.80	-2.19	'1.73 goodnews
0.60	-2.46	1.40	-2.32	2.91	-1.96	1.49	DW = 2.16	'1.91 unemployment
0.59	-3.94	1.01	-3.61	4.50	-2.83	1.93	-1.89	'1.84 political experience
0.56	-2.67	1.22	-3.06	3.98	-2.16	1.44	DW = 2.25	'-1.92 rank among presidents
0.55	-3.97	2.33	-4.33	5.91	-2.15	2.16	-2.54	'-1.45 third party popular vote
0.51	-3.44	1.42	-3.00	4.18	-2.28	1.29	DW = 2.24	'-0.76 delegates

WAR = 1 for 1920, 1944, 1948, 1952, 1968, 1972, 2004, 2008

CANDID = number of candidates nominated at party convention for out of power party

INFLATION: inflation for first 15 quarters of an administration; historical inflation rates for 1914-2016

GROWTH: weighted average real per capita gdp from www.fairmodel.edu

DURATION: 0 if party is in the White House 1 term, 1 (-1) if the Democrat (Republican) occupies the White House two consecutive terms 1.25 (-1.25) three consecutive terms; 1.50 (-1.50) four consecutive terms.

INCUMBENT: 1 if incumbent is running, 0 otherwise

TABLE 5.2. POPULAR VOTE ELECTION FORECAST MODELS. 1900 – 2012

t-statistics for coefficients of variables in the model

	INFLATION	GROWTH	DURATION	INCUMBENT	CANDID	WAR	AR(1)	PERCENTAGE DEMS VOTE
MEDIANS 1992-2012	2.5850	2.0585	0	0	4	0	-0.3748	50.5
MEDIANS 2000-2012	2.3225	1.7265	0	0	2.5	0	-1.7952	51.8
								Constant
Coefficients	-0.8197	0.3426	-6.1589	7.4030	-0.3809	4.4976	-0.4310	53.2706
t-statistics	-4.02	2.01	-3.67	5.01	-2.64	1.93	-1.78	31.51
R-square = 0.66. Durbin-Watson Statistic 1.94 with AR(1).								

t statistics are for AR(1) term unless Durbin-Watson (DW) is close to 2.0 and AR() is unnecessary

SEE TABLE1 FOR INFLATION, GROWTH, DURATION, INCUMBENT, CANDID, WAR

GOODNEWS is number of quarters of administration were GDP growth > 3.2 (see fair)

POLITICAL EXPERIENCE: number of years candidate served in Congress, Vice President or Governor

RANK among Presidents (see Washington Post, 2016b)

THIRD PARTY popular vote (see Matuz, 2015)

DELEGATES: delegates won as a percent of total delegates at the convention for the party not in the White House at the time of the election

DOW AT YEAR-END: election year end Dow Jones Average (see Farrell, 1972, Federal Re-serve Bank of St. Louis, 2016)

TABLE 5.3. 2016 STATEWIDE VOTE PROBIT MODELS

Donald J. Trump vs. Hillary Rodham Clinton

z-statistics for coefficients of variables included in each model

McFadden R-square	PERCAPINC	GDPGR	SENREP	HOUSREP	HISPANIC #	AFRAMER #	POP	AKAIKE IC	ADDITIONAL VARIABLES
0.87	-2.60	-2.05	2.09		-2.49		2.87	0.42	
0.86	-2.67	-1.73		3.66	-1.04			0.39	
0.85	-3.04	-2.07		3.96	0.69	0.69		0.40	
0.70	-3.18	-2.96	3.51			2.05	-0.03	0.64	
0.76	-3.56	-2.44	4.32		-2.24	-2.24	2.75	0.57	
0.78	-3.28	-2.42	3.72		-2.45			0.50	
0.70	-2.98	-2.84	3.49			2.05		0.60	
0.70	-3.18	-2.96	3.51			2.05	-0.03	0.64	
0.79	-3.05	-1.84	3.81		-2.45			0.52	-1.64 HSGRAD
0.78	-2.35	-2.17	3.30		-2.26			0.54	-0.52 BACH
0.78	-3.35	-2.55	3.97		-3.00			0.53	0.79U
0.72	-3.22	-2.84	3.69			2.07		0.62	-1.10U
0.77	-3.56	-3.09	3.79		-2.12	-2.12	2.51	0.60	1.04U
0.78	-3.51	-3.02	3.78		-2.70			0.42	-0.71 SENIORS
0.78	-3.26	-3.43	3.35		-2.39			0.54	0.09 WOMEN

REPWIN is the dependent variable (0,1) measuring whether the state population vote was higher for the Republican (1) or Democrat (0)

PERCAPINC: per capita income in each state

GDPGR: GDP growth rate for each state

SENREP: percentage of the senators that are Republicans for each state

HOUSEREP: percentage of members of the state's delegation in the house that is Republican

HISPANIC: percentage of state population that is Hispanic

AFRAMER: percentage of state population that is African American

POP: number of electoral votes per state

where a z-statistic recorded for both Hispanic and Aframer, the variable is the sum of the percentage of the state population that is either Hispanic or Aframer

CHAPTER 6

ELECTION 2020 : BIDEN BEATS TRUMP[5]

BACKGROUND

Forecasting U.S. presidential elections had become a risky business since "*Dewey Beat Truman.*" Four decades later, it was "certain" that Secretary of State Hillary Clinton would become the first female American President. Four times before 2016, the U.S. popular vote winner was not victorious in the Electoral College.

The 2020 election had aspects that made it particularly interesting. This was the first time a business executive, running as an incumbent, did not have the political experience to maximize the benefits of incumbency.

Trump announced his plan to run for a second term in 2020 almost immediately after he was inaugurated for his first term on January 20, 2017. His predecessors made a considerably greater effort in their first two years in office to assist party members in the Congress to win during the next mid-year election. Trump did little to build Republican Party unity at local, regional, and national levels. Trump's campaign support for other Republican national and local candidates during his time in office was insignificant. As a result, his re-election campaign did not generate as much party loyalty as incumbent presidents usually enjoy. One result was losses by Republican members of the House of Representatives who expected to be re-elected in 2018.

---

[5] This chapter is developed from "Forecasting the 2020 and 2024 U.S. Presidential Elections" published in JOURNAL OF FORECASTING in January 2023. The author thanks John Wiley & Co. for permission to use that material.

The enhancement of the 2020 popular election forecasting model tests the effect of a change in the party that controls the House of Representatives and the Speaker. Others have tested how many seats a party won or lost in midterm elections, having the benefit of occupying the White House, but not whether the speakership had changed parties. The 2018 midterm elections for the House of Representatives changed the speaker from Republican Paul Ryan to Democrat Nancy Pelosi. This change had major effects on the legislation the Trump Administration might enact in the second half of his term and what accomplishments Trump could legitimately claim when he sought re-election.

For 2020, there were unknown effects, including incumbent Trump's medical condition, poor management of COVID-19, and erratic behavior. There were numerous unpredictable impacts, including attempts to reopen the economy too early, voter turnout because of extended voting dates and times, and increased voting by mail. "Benefits" of employing innovative technology were expected, but many election officials were not adequately trained because of COVID-19.

President Trump had expected to run for re-election with a strong macro economy until COVID-19 attacked in March 2020. One year before Election Day 2020, Dmitrieva (2019) cited three highly regarded economic models developed by Ray Fair, Moody's Analytics, and Oxford Economics that predicted Trump's re-election.

Recall that by February 1992, George H. W. Bush had prosecuted a successful War in the Gulf, managed a vibrant economy, and enjoyed highly favorable ratings. Nine months later, the economy had deteriorated (unemployment reached 8 percent, GDP growth declined to -2.2 percent), and Bill Clinton was elected with 43 percent of the popular vote. Bush received 37 percent, and a wealthy, eccentric third-party candidate, H. Ross Perot, received 19 percent.

THE 2020 CANDIDATES

DONALD TRUMP

Donald Trump's business behavior before entering politics is described in Chapter 5. Voters had a clear perspective by November 2020 of whether they would be satisfied with how Trump would behave if he were not re-elected. Before the end of the 2020 campaign, Trump had at least alluded to his plan that if he were not re-elected, he would not accept the result. He claimed weeks before Election Day that he could only be defeated if the voting were rigged against him. No one could have imagined that a sitting President would support an insurrection at the Capitol and that the Vice President's life would be threatened the day the Electoral Votes were being counted.

It was clear that Trump's second-term policies would be more conservative than his first term and that the philosophy of the people he would appoint to surround him would be very conservative. If, for example, a seat on the Supreme Court became vacant during Trump's second term, he would nominate people with views similar to those he appointed in his first term. His supporters approved his choices.

The House of Representatives impeached Donald Trump in December 2019. His first impeachment was for abuse of power, and his second was for soliciting foreign governments to support his campaign. The Senate acquitted him on both charges.

His next impeachment was for active leadership and encouragement of the insurrection on January 6, 2021, after he lost the election to Joe Biden. Trump encouraged his supporters to come to Washington and invade the House of Representatives on the day Vice President Mike Pence opened the Electoral Votes and certified Joe Biden's victory. While the ballots were being counted, rioters broke into House of Representatives offices and conference rooms to destroy government and legislators' personal property. Trump did nothing to discourage the violence by rioters for many hours. Rioters also constructed a hangman's gallows and chanted "Hang Mike Pence." The Committee investigating the January 6 insurrection certified detailed accounts, by witnesses under oath, that President Trump never disavowed these invasions and other illegal activities.

One of Trump's ugliest statements while he was in office occurred when esteemed Republican Senator John McCain died in August of 2018. McCain had been the 2008 Republican candidate for President, a Vietnam War hero and a captive for seven years, and a major Republican Party leader. Trump's comments upon McCain's death did not allude to his service to the nation. Trump referred to McCain's death by saying, "he (Trump) preferred heroes who were alive not dead."

Trump's process for senior executive and cabinet appointments was somewhat unusual. Trump would announce plans to nominate an individual and then appoint the person to an acting position long before forwarding the appointment to the Senate for potential confirmation. These designated appointees served while Trump tested their loyalty to him. If the designee did not exhibit total loyalty to Trump, the appointment was either delayed for a long time or withdrawn before Senate hearings were scheduled.

Members of both political parties were dismayed by Trump's claims to build a wall with Mexico to stop illegal immigrants from entering the U.S. Trump claimed he would build a wall and that Mexico would pay for it. In fact, a few meager miles of wall were constructed and Mexico paid nothing. When the small amount of authorized funds was exhausted, Trump misappropriated funds from several military budgets to support his plans.

JOSEPH BIDEN

Americans knew Joe Biden's behavior would be predictable. The country had known him as a U.S. Senator from Delaware for 36 years, a three-time presidential candidate, and the recent Democratic, two-term (2009-2017) vice president. By 2020, Biden campaigned to be the oldest president in history at age 78.

He was born in a coal-mining region of northeastern Pennsylvania (Scranton, PA) and grew up in northern Delaware. The Bidens were a working-class, devout Catholic family. Joe attended private catholic schools before entering Syracuse

University as an undergraduate and then as a law student. He was a mediocre student.

Biden entered local politics in Wilmington soon after he graduated from law school. He won a U.S. Senate seat at age 29 and served six terms until Barack Obama chose him to be his Vice President. Biden was the ideal partner for President Obama because of his many years in the Senate and the depth of his knowledge of foreign affairs.

Close to the end of his presidency, Obama committed his support to Secretary of State Hillary Clinton (rather than Biden) to run for president in 2016. Biden appeared to be visibly disappointed. From what can be surmised, President Obama may have been concerned about Biden's health. After Biden's son, Beau, returned from serving in Afghanistan, he resumed his position as attorney general for the State of Delaware. He was preparing to announce his campaign to be the next Governor of Delaware when he was diagnosed with cancer. Beau was treated intensively at highly regarded military and private hospitals. He died in May 2015 at about the time Joe Biden would have announced plans and organizations to run for president to succeed President Obama.

Vice President Biden was distraught as any father would be. The Vice President had never recovered from the deaths of his first wife and young daughter, who were killed in an automobile accident three decades ago. Their two sons, Beau and Hunter, were seriously injured, hospitalized for weeks, and eventually were rehabilitated.

Beau's death forced Biden to relive the tragedy of the auto accident. This compromised the Vice President's energy and organization, weakening him as a possible candidate. Many of his potential Democratic opponents had begun organizing and fundraising a year before Beau's death.

Until Biden and the country experienced Trump's conservative policies and his right-wing appointees during his first term, Biden was not planning to enter the 2020 campaign. He had joined a program at the University of Pennsylvania and committed to lucrative engagements as the former U.S. Senator and Vice President. Biden appeared to be ready to retire to private life.

The Democratic Party prevailed on Biden to challenge Trump in 2020 because no other candidate was likely to defeat incumbent Trump. Biden agreed.

COVID-19

In mid-March 2020, COVID-19 attacked the United States. At first, the Trump Administration denied its existence and claimed there were a few minor, unrelated cases. The Administration claimed that premier scientists and disease experts were confusing COVID-19 patients with elderly patients who had other diseases or infirmities. As the epidemic exploded, President Trump suggested several absurd antidotes, such as drinking bleach that people used to whiten their laundry.

Trump hosted a large White House reception after the Senate approved his third Supreme Court appointee, Amy Coney Barrett. Staff and guests were prohibited from wearing masks or applying any potential COVID protection. Many became quite ill. Trump himself and New Jersey Governor Chris Christie both were hospitalized. As more information leaked concerning Trump's hospitalization and the severity of his illness, it became clear that he had been gravely ill and required intense, somewhat risky, experimental treatment.

During the 2020 campaign, Democrats blamed Trump for mishandling COVID-19 (Schiff, 2022; Lemire, 2022; Bowen and Teague, 2022). Seventy-six million people had voted for him in 2016. More than 1.1 million Americans died from COVID-19. For much of 2020, Trump discouraged Americans from wearing masks or accepting free vaccinations despite the recommendations of the experts. In public statements, Trump and many of his Republican colleagues verbally abused infectious disease experts such as Dr. Anthony Fauci. It is certain that some of the 1.1 million deaths could have been prevented with experts' recommended treatments.

Much of the population, perhaps 25 percent of adults, are still unvaccinated in 2024 and rejecting all protection. Boussalis, Coan, and Patel (2011) analyzed the effects of natural disasters on elections across 30 countries between 1880 and 2007, including the Spanish Flu from 1918-1920. They reported that:

"Incumbent parties and leaders are most likely to be punished by voters if (a) the state lacks the capacity or wherewithal to respond appropriately and (b) enough time – but not too much time! – has passed for voters to assign blame to the incumbents."

Abramowitz (2020) suggests that "voters may not hold an incumbent president responsible for a recession brought on by an unforeseeable disaster, like the coronavirus pandemic – although they may hold him responsible for the government's response to the pandemic."

FOUNDATIONS

The foundations for the popular vote election forecasts are previous House of Representative elections, political science studies, and economic models.

House Elections

For 2020, the author investigated whether results from the midyear Congressional elections two years before could help predict the popular vote for the next presidential election. Numerous scholars have suggested that the number of Congressional seat changes could offer insights into future presidential elections. Walker (2023, Appendix A and Table A) confirmed findings by Abramowitz (2016), Campbell (1997, 1991, and 1985), and others that Congressional elections' **seat increases or decreases are not** significant predictors of future presidential elections. Campbell (1991, 1985) argues that causality is the opposite direction from presidential to Congressional elections. Bafumi, Erikson, and Wliezien (2010) recognize that midterm preferences usually shift away from the party in the White House but do not signal "a negative referendum on presidential performance." An incumbent's presidential re-election would have been expected if the incumbent party in the White House held more seats in the House of Representatives after a midterm election than it held four years before the previous midterm election.

The more narrow hypothesis tested here is that a Congressional election that changes the party in control of the

House of Representatives has greater predictive power than counting seat changes. Lewis-Beck and Rice (1992) examined the effects of changes in control of the House of Representatives for 11 presidential elections. Testing the following hypothesis extends their early results.

> H0: Does a mid-term election that changed the party that controlled the leadership of the House or the Senate helps predict the popular vote for the following presidential election?

$$V_t = f[\Delta CONTROL, X] \qquad (6.1)$$

V_t is the Democratic popular vote percentage of the major two-party vote. X is a vector of macroeconomic, behavioral, and structural variables with statistically significant coefficients as determinants of the popular vote.

Taking **new** control brings new leadership to the House or Senate. If a party takes new control in year t-1 and maintains control in year t, the party has strong prospects for enacting new legislation. Republicans held the House majority for 20 of the last 26 years. They have had a tiny majority beginning in January 2023.

Walker (2023, Table A) provides a model with strong statistical significance for coefficients for a change in the House or Senate control preceding a presidential election (1900 – 2016). The independent variables with significant coefficients are the variables in Table 6.1.

Political Science Studies

In 2016, well-known political scientists published studies predicting the popular vote in a special issue of *P.S.: Political Science & Politics* (Ardoin and Gronke, 2016). Their median forecast was that Secretary Clinton would receive 51.1 percent, as she did. Campbell's (2016) trial-heat and economy model and his convention bump and economy model correctly predicted Secretary Clinton's popular vote. Lewis-Beck and Tien (2016) developed a political-economy model that also predicted Clinton would receive 51 percent of the popular vote. Norpoth's (1996, 2020) auto-regressive model forecasts Democratic electoral votes and says, "Trump would defeat Hillary Clinton with 87 percent certainty."

Ten highly regarded political scientists published studies in the fall 2020 issue of *P.S.: Political Science & Politics* (Dassonnville and Tien, 2020) to predict the results of the 2020 presidential election. Their average 2020 popular vote forecast was 47.8 percent for Trump and an Electoral College vote of 237. Trump received 47.8 percent of the popular vote and 232 electoral votes.

Models developed by Enns and Lagodny (2020) and DeSart (2020), 104 days before the election, forecast Electoral College results with little error. Their variables were state economic conditions and presidential approval polls. DeSart had forecasted Trump's 2016 Electoral College victory and a modest popular vote victory.

Economic Models

As discussed in an earlier chapter, Stigler and Fair investigated the effects of macroeconomic factors on presidential elections, motivated by Kramer (1971). Inflation, unemployment, and real income growth are economic factors they argue influence national elections. Fair's model (F) and Walker's enhancement (W) are the basis for the popular vote model in this chapter. The author had predicted five presidential elections' popular votes with an average error of -0.0084 (Walker, 2006 - 2018, and 2000).

Database

This chapter's time-series, cross-section database spans 30 presidential and 51 Congressional midterm elections: 1900 through 2018. The dependent variable is the percentage of the popular vote for Democratic presidential candidate V_t since the Democrats occupied the White House.

POPULAR VOTE MODEL

The popular vote prediction models in the previous chapters established the foundation to predict the popular vote for 2020.

The model is enhanced by testing whether changes in the control of the House of Representatives improve the predictive power of the model. Equation (6.2) is the enhanced model from which Walker (2023) explored numerous alternatives for what terms should be included to examine a change in the control of the House.

V = 53.31-0.82 INFL+5.80 INCUM-0.47CANDID-4.39 TERMS +2.67 WAR+3.02 REP
+4.10 CONTR-0.43 AR(1) --(6.2)

Model H1 is selected from Table 6.1 to predict the 2020 Democratic presidential popular vote because its coefficients have higher t-statistics, the largest adjusted R-square, and the highest F-statistic. Except for WAR, each coefficient is statistically significant at the one percent probability level. The coefficient of WAR is significant at the 10 percent level.

The coefficient of CONTROL (CONTR) of the House is statistically significant at the one percent level. Coefficients for changes in Senate control (S1 and S2) are not significant. Changing the party that controls the Senate is lengthy since only one-third of these seats are elected every two years. Control = 0 for 2020 (no change of leadership for 2018). Democrats' popular vote increases against a Republican incumbent when the country is at war, as Hibbs (2013, 2000) demonstrates with his Bread and Peace models.

Democratic popularity decreases when the party, not the incumbent in the White House, is more unified. Therefore, the party in the White House would have been the Republicans. If a Republican occupies the White House, (REP), has a significant coefficient at the 10 percent level in 7 models.

When INFLATION is included in the model, neither GDP growth nor unemployment has a statistically significant coefficient at even the 20 percent probability level. The coefficient of inflation is always statistically significant. Inflation negatively correlates with Unemployment (-0.41) and War (-0.40). GDP growth is highly correlated (0.69) with a Republican occupying the White House (REP).

In Chapter 5, recall that CANDID measures party unity for the party that does not occupy the White House by the number of candidates nominated at that party's national convention

(CANDID). Biden was the certain Democratic nominee by April 2020, but six other candidates were nominated; Therefore, CANDID = 7. There are various reasons a person may seek to have their name placed in nomination, such as future name recognition, candidates seeking the vice presidency, or people planning to run for president four years later, although when the nominee is already known.

The classic case was when John Kennedy appeared to seek the nomination for vice president in 1956. He withdrew with the stipulation that his brother Bobby would be guaranteed a seat on Presidential nominee Ali Stevenson's presidential campaign airplane. At the end of the campaign had developed 50 large notebooks that became Kennedy's strategy to run for president in 1960.

POPULAR VOTE FORECAST

Walker's forecasts for the 2020 popular vote were developed and published (Walker 2020, SSRN) in the summer of 2020. Equation (6.2) is the empirical model from Table 6.1, line H1. The Democratic popular vote is forecast when CONTROL = 1, REP =1, WAR = 0, CANDID = 7, INCUMBENT = 0, DURATION = 1, and INFLATION = 1.1 on Election Day (*The Economist,* November 7, 2020, page 78). Whether a Republican occupies the White House (REP) has a significant coefficient at the 10 percent level in 7 models. Equation (6.2) predicts Biden's share of the two-party popular vote would be 52.7 percent. It was 52.2.

The poll of poll averages at the end of October 2020 predicted Biden would receive 55 percent of the two-party vote. That forecast was developed to reduce the effects of extreme values above or below the average. Zitner (2021) and Balz (2021) delineate that popular vote presidential polling for 2020 was the least accurate in the past 40 years.

ELECTORAL COLLEGE PROBIT MODEL

To develop the model to forecast the Electoral College, the dependent variable is REP2020 ST, which has a value of 1 if Trump won the state in 2016 or a value of 0 if he lost the state.

The first quarter of 2020 state income growth is employed as a proxy for state GDP growth because COVID-19 provided unreliable first-quarter growth rates.

2016 Electoral College Model

Recall that after the 2016 presidential election, the estimated equation, repeated here as Equation (6.3), was developed by the author to understand Trump's Electoral College victory with a 50-state cross-section probit model. The dependent, binary variable is whether President Trump won the state's 2016 popular vote. The cross-section 50-state (ST) probit model explains Trump's 2016 state electoral win (1) or loss (0), (REP 2016 ST).

REP 2016 ST = 44.56 – .0016 ST per capita - 1.5005 %Δ ST + .0815 % ST REP
State win = 1   [2.83]   [-2.75]   income   [-2.11] GDP   [2.18] senators
State loss = 0   (.005)   (.006)   (.035)   (.029)

   -.3246 % Hispanic ST population   + .0003 ST population   (6.3)
   [-2.67]   [2.97]
   (.008)   (.003)

2020 Electoral College Forecast

The 2020 Electoral College vote is forecast for each state (REP 2020 ST), inputting 2020 state data into Equation (6.3) for the independent variables. REP 2020 ST scores appear in the first data column of Table 6.3. The aggregate mean is subtracted from each state score to normalize the REP 2020 data to zero. The transformed mean and standard deviation are 0 and 1.9, respectively. When a state's adjusted score is positive (i.e. REP 2020 ST>0), Trump is forecast to win the state's electoral votes. If REP 2020 ST is negative (REP 2020 ST < 0), Biden is predicted to win the state's electoral votes.

The second column in Table 6.3 equals 1 if Trump is forecast to win the state in 2020. The third column is 1 if Trump won the state in 2016. The right-hand column represents Trump's expected state electoral vote difference between the 2020 forecast and 2016 data. Positive values predict 2020 Trump gains, and negative values forecast 2020 Trump losses.

Trump was predicted to lose states with a total of 74 electoral votes in 2020, which he had won in 2016. Maine was forecast to give Trump a popular vote state majority and one Congressional district in Maine. Trump also was predicted to win four of the five Electoral Votes in Nebraska. He was predicted to lose the one Nebraska Electoral Vote for the Congressional district for Omaha. Twenty-eight electoral votes for Alaska, New Mexico, and Pennsylvania were forecast to be won by Biden. Forty-six electoral votes for Texas, Wyoming, and Nebraska were forecast for Biden because of their sizable Hispanic populations; however, approximately 50 percent did not vote in 2016, and the same Hispanic percentage was expected to vote in 2020. All three states have Republican voting histories in national elections.

ELECTORAL COLLEGE PROBIT FORECAST

The forecast of 46 votes for Biden from Texas, Wyoming, and Nebraska (38, 3, and 5, respectively) are reallocated to Trump. Therefore, states with positive scores in Table 6.3 would provide Trump with 282 electoral votes (236 + 46) and Biden with 256 (302 − 46). The analysis begins with Trump having 236 Electoral Votes and Biden having 256.

Ten states forecast for Biden with 71 Electoral Votes (Panel A, Table 6.4) and 8 states forecast for Trump with 67 Electoral Votes (Panel B, Table 6.4) require more in-depth analysis. To win, Biden needed to win the 45 electoral votes from Wisconsin (10), Michigan (15), and Pennsylvania (20), which he won. As an alternative, Biden needed to win at least two states from among Wisconsin (10), Iowa (6), Utah (6), and Kansas (6), which he did not receive. Several illustrative scenarios, beginning with 282 votes for Trump and 256 votes for Biden, follow:

(i) Biden winning Wisconsin, Michigan, and Pennsylvania (he did)

      Biden 256 + 10 (WI) + 15 (MI) + 20 (PA) = 301

      Trump 282 − 10 (WI) - 15 (MI) − 20 (PA) = 237

               Biden elected

(ii) Biden winning Michigan and one Congressional district in Nebraska (he did)

      Biden 256 + 15 (MI) + 1 (NE) = 272

      Trump 282 − 15 (MI) - 1 (NE) = 266

Biden elected
(iii) Biden winning Michigan and two votes in Maine (he did)
Biden   256 + 15 (MI)   + 2 (MA) = 273
Trump 282 – 15 (MI)   - 2 (MA) = 265
Biden elected

Biden was victorious by winning several states in 2020, which Trump had won by narrow margins in 2016. In 2020, Republicans were disappointed to lose the 16 electoral votes from Georgia and 11 from Arizona, which were not conceded until fall 2021 (Helderman, 2021). The result for 2020 was 306 Electoral Votes for Biden and 232 Electoral Votes for Trump.

CONCLUSIONS

The 2020 two-party popular vote is forecast by re-estimating the time-series model to include 2016 presidential election year data (1900 – 2016). A change in political control of the House of Representatives during the 2018 mid-year Congressional elections strengthens the popular vote forecast model. The enhanced Walker model has strong statistical test statistics.

Biden was forecast to win 52.7 of the popular vote, which was adjusted to 52.2 percent for the dual incumbency. He won 52.2 percent of the popular vote. *The values for the independent variables were assumed on December 1, 2022, which was quite risky.* The re-estimated 50-state, cross-section, probit model includes state data through 2016. The revised models forecast that Trump would win the 2020 Electoral College unless Democrats won all of Pennsylvania, Michigan, and Wisconsin, which they did. The three scenarios – (i), (ii), and (iii) – were not far from the actual result of Biden winning 306 Electoral Votes and Trump winning 232.

TABLE 6.1: CHANGE OF CONGRESSIONAL CONTROL

	Adj. Rsq./ STAT	CONST	INFLAT	DUR	INCUM	CANDID	WAR	REPUB	HOUSE	HOU*	SENATE	SEN*	AR(1) DW
H1	0.75	53.3058	-0.8236	-4.3870	5.7996	-0.4738	2.6724	3.0212	**4.1009**				1.94
	11.35	(38.66)*	(-5.43)*	(-3.86)*	(5.39)*	(-4.57)*	(1.77)#	(2.11)+	(3.55)*				2.13
H2	0.76	52.2129	-0.7696	-4.7234	5.8907	-0.2864	2.9273	4.1432	6.1669	-0.3502			-2.72
	10.73	(34.54)*	(-5.27)*	(-4.38)*	(6.07)*	(-1.76)#	(2.06)+	(2.73)*	(3.10)*	(-1.39)			2.26
S1	0.64	55.7558	-0.7890	-4.2169	4.4672	-0.5335	2.8706	3.0451			3.1044		2.47
	7.15	(39.24)*	(-4.43)*	(-3.07)*	(3.04)*	(-4.21)*	(1.64)	(1.72)#			(1.83)#		1.81
S2	0.62	55.5434	-0.7438	-4.4457	4.6142	-0.5175	3.1590	3.3767			3.7721	-0.1067	-2.62
	6.11	(36.17)*	(-3.60)*	(-2.99)+	(3.03)*	(-3.86)*	(1.66)	(1.76)#			(1.62)	(-0.42)	1.82

INFLATION is the rate of inflation for the first 15 months of the election year. DURATION = 0 if the party is in the White House 1 term, 1 (-1) if the Democrat (Republican) occupies the White House two consecutive terms; 1.25 (-1.25) three consecutive terms; 1.50 (-1.50) four consecutive terms. INCUMBENT = 1 if an incumbent is running, 0 otherwise.

CANDID = number of candidates nominated at the party convention for the party out of power. WAR =1 for 1920, 1944, 1948, 1952, 1968, 1972, 2004, 2008. REP = 1 if there is a Republican president. HOUSE or SENATE measures the hypothesized change.

* significant at the .001 level	+ significant at the .05 level	# significant at the .10 level	

TABLE 6.2: DEMOCRATIC 2020 POPULAR VOTE MODEL

VARIABLE	DEFINITION	VALUE	COEFFICIENT (t-statistic)
CONSTANT	INTERCEPT	1.0	53.3058 (38.66)*
INFLATION	ANNUAL INFLATION	1.1	-0.8236 (-6.43)*
INCUMBENT	INCUMBENT RUNNING No = 0, Yes 1	1.0	5.7996 (5.39)*
CANDID	CANDIDATES NOMINATED	8	-0.4738 (-4.47)*
DURATION	NUMBER OF TERMS INCUMBENT SERVED	1	-4.3870 (-3.86)*
WAR	COUNTRY AT WAR No =0, Yes =1	0	2.6724 (1.77)#
REP. PRES.	REPUBLICAN OCCUPIES WHITE HOUSE: No =0, Yes =1	1	3.0212 (2.11)+
CONTROL	DID PARTY CONTROLLING HOUSE CHANGE @ t-2 No = 0, Yes = 1	0	4.1009 (3.55)*
AR(1)	FORECAST ERROR CORRECTION	0.84	-0.4326 (-1.94)+
R-SQ/ ADJ. R-SQ			0.82 / 0.75
F STAT / DW			11.35 / 2.13
2020 DEMOCRAT PREDICTED POPULAR VOTE			52.7
Adjusted to account for dual incumbency.			52.2
*SIGNIFICANT AT THE .01 LEVEL + SIGNIFICANT AT THE .05 LEVEL # SIGNIFICANT AT THE .10 LEVEL			

TABLE 6.3: 2020 ELECTORAL COLLEGE FORECAST

STATE	2020 REPWIN SCORE	2020 REP WIN	2016 REP WIN	ELECTORS	2020 MINUS 2016	
ALABAMA	2.21	1	1	9	0	
ALASKA	-2.58	0	1	3	-3	
ARIZONA	0.89	1	1	11	0	
ARKANSAS	2.89	1	1	6	0	
CALIFORNIA	-2.87	0	0	55	0	
COLORAD.	-1.40	0	0	9	0	
CONNECT	-3.04	0	0	7	0	
DELAW.	-2.27	0	0	3	0	
FLORIDA	1.96	1	1	29	0	
GA	1.09	1	1	16	0	
HAWAII	-0.74	0	0	4	0	
IDAHO	2.27	1	1	4	0	
ILLINOIS	-1.52	0	0	20	0	
INDIANA	1.62	1	1	11	0	
IOWA	0.26	1	1	6	0	
KANSAS	0.48	1	1	6	0	
KENTUCKY	2.59	1	1	8	0	
LOUISANIA	1.08	1	1	8	0	
MAINE	1.85	1	0	4	3	
MD	-1.50	0	0	10	0	
MASS	-4.27	0	0	11	0	
MICHIGAN	1.02	1	1	15	0	
MINNESOTA	-1.16	0	0	10	0	
MISSISS	3.71	1	1	6	0	
MISSOURI	1.81	1	1	10	0	
MONTANA	1.88	1	1	3	0	
NEBRASKA	-0.69	0	1	5	-5	

STATE	2020 REPWIN SCORE	2020 REP WIN	2016 REP WIN	ELECTORS	2020 MINUS 2016	
NEVADA	-0.04	0	0	6	0	
NH	-0.58	0	0	4	0	
NJ	-1.93	0	0	14	0	
N MEXICO	-0.83	0	0	5	0	
NY	-3.16	0	0	29	0	
N CAROLINA	1.48	1	1	15	0	
N DAKOTA	-2.15	0	1	3	-3	
OHIO	0.84	1	1	18	0	
OK	0.96	1	1	7	0	
OREGON	-0.19	0	0	7	0	
PA	-0.08	0	1	19	-19	
RI	-0.33	0	0	4	0	
S CAROLINA	2.51	1	1	9	0	
S DAKOTA	0.74	1	1	3	0	
TENN	1.68	1	1	11	0	
TEXAS	-1.22	0	1	38	-38	
UTAH	0.46	1	1	6	0	
VERMONT	-2.49	0	0	3	0	
VA	-0.84	0	0	13	0	
WASH	-2.90	0	0	12	0	
W VA	2.57	1	1	5	0	
WISCON	0.45	1	1	10	0	
WYOMING	-0.96	0	1	3	-3	
DC	-3.06	0	0	3	0	
MEAN=	0.0	SD=		1.9		SUM=69

TABLE 6.4: 2020 STATES FORECAST TO BE CLOSE

PANEL A: Forecast for Biden			PANEL B: Forecast for Trump		
States	2020 REP score*	electoral votes	States	2020 REP score*	electoral votes
NEVADA	-0.04	6	IOWA	0.26	6
PA	-0.08	20	WISCONSIN	0.45	10
OREGON	-0.19	7	UTAH	0.46	6
RI	-0.33	4	KANSAS	0.48	6
NH	-0.58	4	S. DAKOTA	0.74	3
NE	-0.68	5(2+3)	OHIO	0.84	18
HAWAII	-0.74	4	ARIZONA	0.89	11
N. MEXICO	-0.83	5	OKLA	0.96	7
VIRGINIA	-0.84	13			
WYOMIING	-0.96	3			
TOTAL		71	TOTAL		67
% of 538		13.20%	% OF 538		12.45%
TEXAS	-1.22	38	MICHIGAN	1.02	15
			GEORGIA	1.09	16
			MAINE	1.85	4(2+2)

CHAPTER 7

DEMOCRACY FORECASTS FOR 2024[6]

INTRODUCTION

The major changes in this Chapter on July 22, 2024 versus the forecast in the January 2023 publication of the *Journal of Forecasting* are in the section on Immeasurables and Unpredictables and the first subsection of the CONCLUSIONS.

The author's forecast is that Vice President Harris and her running mate, Minnesota Governor Tim Walz will be elected in November.

BACKGROUND

Forecasting U.S. presidential elections had become a risky business since *"Dewey Beat Truman."* Four decades later, it was "certain" that Secretary of State Hillary Clinton would become the first female American President. Four times before 2016, the U.S. popular vote winner was not victorious in the Electoral College.

The 2020 election had aspects that made it particularly interesting. This was the first time a business executive, running as an incumbent, did not have the political expertise to maximize the benefits of incumbency.

Trump announced his plan to run for a second term in 2020 almost immediately after he was inaugurated for his first term on January 20, 2017. His predecessors made a considerably greater effort in their first two years in office to assist party members in the Congress to win during the next mid-year election. Trump did little

---

[6] This chapter is developed from "Forecasting the 2020 and 2024 U.S. Presidential Elections" published in JOURNAL OF FORECASTING in January 2023. The author thanks John Wiley & Co. for their permission to use that material.

to build Republican Party unity at local, regional, and national levels. Trump's campaign support for other Republican national and local candidates during his office years was insignificant. As a result, his re-election campaign did not generate as much party loyalty as incumbent presidents usually enjoy. One result was losses by Republican members of the House of Representatives who expected to be re-elected in 2018.

The enhancement of the 2020 popular election forecasting model tests the effect of a change in the party that controls the House of Representatives and the Speaker. For 2024, the enhancements are to include women's choice as an important forecasting variable and recognize the "dual" incumbency in the 2024 presidential election.

The 2024 popular vote and the Electoral College forecasts are developed beyond the January 2023 publication. An auto-regressive time-series regression model is employed to predict the popular vote. A much enhanced cross-section probit model is applied to forecast the Electoral College vote.

PREPARATION FOR 2024

Democratic Preparations

Early in Biden's presidential term, the Administration negotiated a $1.9 trillion COVID-19 relief bill - the American Rescue Plan, enacted on March 11, 2021. The Administration proposed a separate $1 trillion infrastructure bill to support the President's economic and social agenda, issued 41 executive orders, and reversed some Trump policies.

The Biden Administration contended with new and continuing challenges from its first day in office. There were new major outbreaks of the COVID-19 virus, especially where citizens rejected free vaccinations. More than 1.1 million Americans died. Some conservative public officials argue that it was unnecessary to wear masks, unwise to accept free vaccinations, and ineffective to close schools and places of business.

The Administration gained an immediate appreciation for the long-run global warming issues. Providing timely assistance to hurricane victims in Florida, South Carolina, New Jersey, Texas, Louisiana, Puerto Rico, and Haiti was essential.

Immigration policies continue to be controversial and confusing. In May 2024, some *Republicans in the House of Representatives refused to support the immigration bill that had broad support after Trump opposed the bill. On June 5, 2024, President Biden issued an executive order with similar content to the legislation.* He preferred to have the Congress enact legislation.

By the summer of 2022, the Democrats' prospects for the midterm elections appeared bleak. Many experts predicted the Democrats would lose control of both the Senate and House of Representatives by large margins. Expectations changed somewhat after the Inflation Reduction Act of 2022 was enacted on August 13. The Act provided many of the components proposed 18 months before as part of the $1 trillion Build Back Better legislation.

The title of the 2022 legislation was misleading. It dealt with some aspects of climate change, modernized the IRS somewhat, increased taxes on those earning more than $400,000 and large corporations' profits, and reduced costs of prescription drugs covered by Medicare. The final budget was $739 billion.

The Supreme Court rejected the Administration's comprehensive plan to reduce students' debt obligations. The Administration reduced some of the student debt obligations via executive orders that separated student debt into categories.

Republican's 2024 Preparation

Donald Trump announced his candidacy for the 2024 presidency one week after the November 2022 midterm election. His party leadership and nomination were hardly challenged. None of Trump's challengers came close to beating him in a primary. His activities since his 2000 defeat are indicative of what to expect if he wins another term.

Trump will be engaged by several Federal and state courts in trials and appeals that will continue for many years. In May 2024, in the Federal Court for the Southern District of New York, a jury of 12 New Yorkers convicted him of 34 counts of illegal business practices. The judge, whom Trump interrupted and criticized continually during the trial, will impose the sentence in September for his 34 convictions.

In Florida, Trump held important, classified, and secret documents at Mar-a—Lago, moving them from the White House with no authority. He refused to cooperate with the FBI's efforts to recapture the documents. The case in Georgia is transparent because Trump's telephone call to state officials was recorded. Trump requested officials to increase his state's popular vote total by almost 12,000 votes so that he would win Georgia. The original results that Trump lost Georgia were correct and were verified numerous times. The third case is the federal case in which Trump is charged with encouraging the January 6, 2021, Washington, DC, insurrection at the Capitol. After violence had continued for several hours, Trump's family and staff prevailed on him to make a public statement asking rioters to leave the Capitol.

On July 1, the Supreme Court ruled that a president cannot be prosecuted for an action that is part of a presidential duty. For an indictment of a president, a court will have to decide whether the action was or was not part of a presidential duty. This followed the Court's June 28 ruling reducing the Justice Department's authority to prosecute charges of obstruction of justice from the January 6 insurrection.

Some of Trump's supporters may change their views because of his convictions in New York, his anti-Semitic statements, and numerous other indictments. A few Republicans and independents are not happy with Trump's behavior during the January 6 insurrection.

Trump continues to repeat the Big Lie (Lemire, 2022), saying that "he won the presidency" in 2020. His policy, separating very young immigrant children from their parents at the southern border, offends many Americans when they understand the details. (Baker and Glasser, 2022, chapter 12).

If Trump were elected in 2024, he may withdraw American support from the Ukraine and negotiate with Russia to settle the war. He stated that he would withdraw the U.S. from many international organizations, as he had done during his first term. Trump has announced he would not defend NATO members who are in arrears for their financial obligations. As a summary of his intentions, he claims publicly that he would like to be a dictator.

2024 Recession

After two-quarters of negative GDP growth in 2020, the economy grew 2.9 percent in the third quarter (revised upward from 2.6) while unemployment remained at 3.9 percent. For the first and second quarters of 2024, there are few signs of a recession, and inflation declined by 0.1 percent *(The Economist, July 20, 2024, p.73)*. Many economists expected a recession to result from the government's high expenses to fight COVID, the increasing fiscal deficits and debt, and the substantial U.S. support for both Israel and the Ukraine. Larry Summers (Tully, 2022) argued that the Fed would need to maintain a real Fed funds target rate as high as 5.5 percent to reduce inflation. Summers has been correct, and Federal Reserve Chairman Powell agrees. The July 2024 rate is between 5.25 and 5.50 percent.

The July 2024 U.S. inflation rate, measured by the Consumer Price Index, declined to 3.0 percent and is projected to be 3.0 percent for the year (The Economist, July 20, 2024, p.73). The Treasury bill's 6-month rate is 4.70 percent and the 10-year Treasury securities' rate is 4.38 percent. (Wall Street Journal, August 6, p. B8). An inverted yield curve, where the short-term rate is above the long-term rate, suggests there could be a recession in the near future. After the July, 2024 FOMC meeting, Chairman Powell stated that the Fed might reduce the target rates in the fall. The FOMC did not have the August 2 employment data for this meeting.

Professor Ray Fair has shown that the performance of the macroeconomy during a presidential election year has a major impact on the election, but the economy for previous years is hardly remembered. The average length of an American recession is 18 months (NBER, 2021). If a recession had begun any time in 2023, it probably would not have ended before Election Day 2024, and it could have determined the outcome of the election.

ECONOMIC ENVIRONMENT

FED Policy

In the spring of 2021, Federal Reserve Chair Jerome Powell expected to keep short-term interest rates low through 2022 and that the Fed might taper its support for the economy before 2023 (Powell, *The Washington Post,* April 28, 2021). At the beginning of 2022, the Fed Funds rate was less than one-half of one percent. By summer, inflation was rampant, and year-over-year consumer price increases reached 9.3 percent (*The Economist,* August 13, 2022, page 76). Two years later, inflation had declined to 3.0 percent.

Chairman Powell pursued the successful policy that Paul Volgker had employed in 1981, substantially increasing target short-term interest rates. Powell's Federal Reserve Open Market Committee (FOMC) raised short-term target rates three times in the first three quarters of 2022. After the September 2022 FOMC meeting, Chairman Powell predicted the target short-term rates could be 4.25 percent by year-end 2022 and 4.6 percent by the end of 2023 (Timiraos, *The Wall Street Journal, September 22, 2022*). By Thanksgiving (Timiraos, The *Wall Street Journal, November 3, 2022*), the Fed raised the target range to 3.75 – 4.00 percent. Speaking at the Brookings Institution on August 25, 2023, Powell stated that rates may be raised again in December, but the increase could be smaller than he had expected. By October, inflation declined to 7.7 percent (*The Economist, November 26,* 2022, page 75).

Democrat's Economy

The U.S. economy has recovered from a volatile period. For the first 42 months of the Administration, there was no choice but to implement huge public expenditures to stimulate the economy and accept the necessary inflation (up to 9 percent) that accompanied the reopening of the economy after the COVID-19 effects. It was essential for the Administration to provide considerable financial support for many people, businesses, and schools affected by COVID-19. More than 100 million Americans suffered from the disease. Many people had COVID more than once, and many cases were never reported.

For 2023 and 2024, economic forecasters expected inflation to be approximately 3 percent and unemployment to be less than 4 percent. For the first quarter of 2024, inflation was 3.0 percent, unemployment was 4.1 percent, and GDP growth was 2.9 percent (The Economist, June 1, 2024, p. 73). One indicator that inflation is declining during the second half of 2024 is the decline in the 6-month Treasury Bill rate from 5.20 to 4.70 between July 15th and August 5, respectively (Wall Street Journal, July 23, p. B11 and Wall Street Journal, , August 6, p. B8, respectively).

Popular Vote Forecast Equation

The 2022 midterm elections revealed voters' concerns. Young voters went to the polls in record numbers. Democracy, women's choice for their health decisions, and inflation were the major issues.

The 2024 Democratic popular vote is forecast from Equation (7.1). This equation

$$V = 53.66 - 0.88\ \text{INFL} + 5.68\ \text{INCUM} - 0.48\ \text{CANDID} - 3.78\ \text{TERMS} + 2.37\ \text{WAR}$$
$$+ 2.68\ \text{REP} + 3.99\ \text{CONTROL} - 0.44\ \text{AR(1)} \text{--} (7.1)$$

has the same form as Equation (6.1), after including 2020 data. The coefficients and test statistics are re-estimated but are not different. The far-right column of Table 7.1 provides coefficients with t-statistics in parentheses. Each coefficient is statistically different from zero at the 5 percent probability level, except the coefficients of WAR and when a Republican is president, which are significant at the 10 percent level. The F-statistic is 11.43; the adjusted R-square is 0.74; and the Durbin-Watson statistic is 2.24.

2024 POPULAR VOTE FORECAST

Candid (Republican nominees)

CANDID measures the competitive environment for the nomination for the party that is not the incumbent. Trump did not allow nominations, other than himself. Former U.S.

Representative to the UN Nikki Haley could have asked her delegates to nominate her as a show of force for 2028. Other nominees could have included women opposing the Supreme Court's decision on Roe v. Wade. Often states nominate a "favorite son" to gain visibility. People who seek consideration for a potential position in a Trump Administration could have sought a nomination. Candidates who will campaign for a major federal or state office in the future are often nominated to gain visibility.

The Democrats unified behind Biden before their summer 2020 national convention. However, six other candidates were nominated at that convention. For 2024, CANDID = 5 is a reasonable assumption, if Trump had permitted nominees.

Inflation

Inflation is the most important macroeconomic variable that affected the 2022 midterm election, and it will be a critical concern for voters in 2024 (Stigler, 1973; Fair 2020a, Walker 2023). Before November 2024, the incumbent administration must convince voters that inflation is under control and was caused by the costs of COVID-19. After the June and July FOMC meetings, Chairman Powell said he hoped the Fed could reduce target interest rates again this year (*The Washington Post, 2024, June 13 and The Washington Post, 2024, July 31,respectively*).

Voters surely know the source of the 2021-2023 inflation. Much of the early inflation under Biden resulted from the essential government assistance to respond to COVID-19 or to be protected from the disease.

Control of the House

Midterm 2022 Congressional elections changed the control and leadership of the House of Representatives to the Republicans by a tiny margin. On January 3, 2023, when the 435 members of the 118th House of Representatives were sworn in, Republican Congressman Kevin McCarthy (R-CA) was elected Speaker to replace Democratic Congresswoman Nancy Pelosi (D-CA). Speaker McCarthy was not a popular choice; it required 16 ballots for McCarty to be elected. After a few months, his party rejected him. After having a temporary speaker for approximately ten weeks, Mike Johnson, a relatively unknown Congressman from Louisiana, was selected as a compromise speaker. Sometimes Speaker Johnson has required House Democrats' votes to complete rudimentary administrative tasks.

Dual Incumbency

In 1892, Grover Cleveland, the 22nd President, was elected as the 24th president. Following his first term, 1885 -1889, Benjamin Harrison defeated Cleveland in 1888. Harrison's weak leadership (1889 – 1893) diminished any value of his incumbency. In 1892, Cleveland defeated incumbent Harrison. Harrison and Cleveland could have been considered incumbents for the 1892 presidential election.

Other Issues

Additional potential effects on the popular vote are tested by introducing binary variables to Equation (7.1). The 19th Amendment to the Constitution guaranteed women the right to vote. A coefficient to test voting differences before and after the enactment of the 19th Amendment was not statistically different from 0. Another binary variable represented the 50 years, 1972-2022, when women had "choice" versus the years before 1972. The coefficient of this binary variable is not statistically significant at any meaningful level.

Known November Values for Independent Variables

November values for some variables in Equation (7.1) are already known. Democrats occupy the White House (REP = 0), they are incumbents (INCUM = 1), and they are serving their first term (DURATION = 1). President Biden has pledged not to engage in a traditional ground War (WAR = 0) while continuing to support the Ukraine and Israel. The party controlling the House of Representatives and the Speaker's party changed due to the 2022 midterm election. (CONTROL = 1).

<u>2024 Popular Vote Prediction</u>

The author's forecast for the 2024 popular vote appears in Table 7.1, based on data available until December 1, 2022. The prediction was that **53.7 percent of the popular vote** would favor the Democratic candidate. *Donald Trump had not yet become the Republicans' presumed 2024 nominee.*

*Incumbency contributes 5.68 percent to the 53.7 percent forecast since 5.68 is the coefficient of incumbency in Equation (7.1). Some portion of this coefficient may be reduced because of the 2024 dual incumbency for both candidates. The author's opinion is that one-third of the 5.68 coefficient should be reduced for dual incumbency. When a party does not have an incumbent, it must invest significant resources so voters recognize their candidate. The Democrat's predicted popular vote is **51.8 (53.7 – (.33 x 5.68))**.*

Table 7.2 WEIGHTED INCUMBENT DILUTION

C	1.0	.33	.50	.67	0
V(2024)	53.7	51.8	50.9	50.6	48.0

2024 ELECTORAL VOTE FORECAST

<u>Party Organization and Conventions</u>

Party Organization: *According to media reports, the Republican Party state organizations were in chaos in Nevada, Arizona, and Michigan six months before the election. This becomes important when the parties begin to focus on voter turnout. There is no substitute for distributing flyers, knocking on doors, telephoning neighbors, and offering transportation to the polls on Election Day.*

Conventions: *Local politicians and business leaders enjoy the benefits of hosting a national party nominating convention. The revenues, media coverage, and other benefits are enjoyed for decades. In 2024, Republicans celebrated their nominating convention in Milwaukee, Wisconsin, in July, and Democrats will convene their nominating convention in August in Chicago, Illinois.*

The order of the party's conventions alternates between presidential election years.

Chicago is a somewhat risky choice for the Democrats because some people, and surely the media, will recall the riots, demonstrations, and mass arrests at the 1972 Democratic Convention. Thousands of people protested the War in Vietnam. In 2020, Milwaukee, Wisconsin, hosted the Democrats, and Charlotte, North Carolina, hosted the Republicans.

ROE v. WADE

In June 2022, the U. S. Supreme Court reversed its 1973 ruling on Roe v. Wade. The reversal made women's reproductive choice illegal nationwide, **unless** a state enacts specific legislation to the contrary. The three conservative Supreme Court Justices whom Trump nominated led the reversal.

Spring 2024 surveys report that 55 percent of the population disagrees with the Court. Since the 2024 presidential election is the first one since the 2020 ruling, Women's Choice has become an increasingly important issue. Trump agrees with the court ruling but is wavering and suggesting that it could be a state issue rather than a federal one. Harris and Biden vigorously disagree with the Court.

CHOICE

Twenty states currently allow women to choose a form of birth control or to have an abortion. Specific circumstances vary among states. There will be proposed changes on numerous 2024 state ballots. With Kamala Harris as the Democratic presidential nominee, Choice will be emphasized as a major Democrats' campaign issue.

To measure the level of CHOICE, for the state's position, each state is assigned a score (1, 3, 5, or 7).

CHOICE = 1, a state allows women no choice, 15 states

CHOICE = 3, a state allows women to have choice up to 15 days of pregnancy, 5 states

CHOICE = 5, a state allows women to have choice up to 26 days of pregnancy,9 states

CHOICE = 7, a state allows women total choice, 21 states

<u>Probit Model</u>

An enhanced probit model is estimated to predict a state's electoral vote. The binary dependent variable (REPWIN24) measures whether Republicans (REPWIN24 = 1) or Democrats (REPWIN24 = 0) are expected to win a particular state. Equation, (7.2), is an enhanced probit model that includes CHOICE, after the 2022 Court's ruling.

REPWIN 2024 = 21.99 – .0004 ST per capita + 1.2456 %Δ ST + .0613 % ST REP
   State win = 1 [4.18] [-3.92]   income   [2.09] GDP [2.76] senators
   State loss = 0 (.000) (.000)   (.037)   (.006)

    + .0003 ST population   - .9993 CHOICE --- (7.2)
       [3.20]   [-2.81]
       (.001)   (.005)

The enhanced probit model for 2024 has five *independent variables. Four variables continue from the author's 2016 model: state per capita income and GDP growth,* a state's Federal leadership -- the party of the state's U.S. Senators -- and state population. Three of the four variables have stronger statistical test results, and the test for the fourth variable is unchanged.

Since the original model was developed in 2016, the definition and measure of a state's Hispanic population have become increasingly ambiguous because of changing self-identification and complex immigration issues. When the Hispanic state population is included in the enhanced model, its coefficient is not statistically significantly different from zero at any meaningful level.

CHOICE is tested as an alternative fifth variable. Its coefficient is negative and statistically significantly different from zero at the 0.001 probably level. Women's CHOICE has an inverse relationship to REPWIN24. If a state increases (decreases) Woman's CHOICE, the predicted value of REPWIN24 decreases (increases).

The probit equation, (7.2), forecasts values for REPWIN 2024. The equation has the same strong test statistics as the version developed in 2016. Numbers in parentheses () reflect the small probability that a coefficient is zero. The z statistics, in brackets [ ] are analogous to t-statistics for large samples or populations. They test whether coefficients are statistically different from zero. The McFadden R-square is 0.87, and the AKAIKE criterion is 0.42.

State Histories and Forecasting

Predicting the 2024 Electoral College vote has two components to evaluate for each state. **First**, a probit model score is calculated to distinguish the seven states, often called swing states, which are predicted to be highly competitive campaigns. The other 43 states ARE NOT expected to have highly contested campaigns.

Second, a state-by-state case analysis is necessary to predict outcomes for the seven highly competitive states. After subtracting the 0.81 mean to center the values on 0, the resulting scores are denoted as REPFOR in Table 7.3 in the far-right column. The author's prediction of which party will win the state's electoral votes is labeled PARTY in Table 7.3.

A party that won a state's 2020 popular vote <u>by more than five percentage</u> points or with a large absolute value probit forecast score expects victory in 2024. With modest resource commitments in those 43 states, Republicans expect to win, 193 Electoral Votes, and Democrats expect to win 222 Electoral Votes. The other seven states' have modest probit scores and 93 Electoral Votes.

Republicans:	193 electoral votes
Democrats:	222 electoral votes
7 States with less than 5%	
2020 Popular Vote Differences:	93 electoral votes
Or a small REPFOR	

Florida's 30 Electoral Votes are added to the 193 Republican votes because it is Trump's home, and the state has become considerably more conservative in recent years. The state's governor and both U.S. Senators are Republicans. Thus, the 2024 Electoral College forecast begins with

Republicans:	193 + 30 **(FL)** =	223 electoral votes
Democrats:	=	222 electoral votes

7 States with less than 5%
2020 Popular Vote Differences: 93 electoral votes
Or a small REPFOR

Vice President Harris selected Minnesota Governor Tim Walz as her running mate who should appeal to voters from some of the 7 States with less than 5 percent of the 2020 Popular Vote Differences or with a small REPFOR in Table 7.3. She is well acquainted with most of the Democratic governors.

President Trump had chosen 39-year-old Ohio Senator J D Vance to be his running mate. Vance has offended many single and married people who do not have children.

Voting in the Seven States

North Carolina (NC) historically votes Republican, and the 2020 Republican convention was held in Charlotte (Anderson and Svrluga, 2021). Since 1980, the state has only voted for the Democratic presidential candidate once.

The Board of Directors for the University at North Carolina at Chapel Hill, the state's flagship university, rejected tenure applications for two African-American co-authors of the well-known book *1619, which focused on African American history and culture. The Board* supposedly represents the state's population in reviewing academic appointments. Adding North Carolina's electoral votes to the Republican total provides

Republicans 223 + 16 **(NC)** = 239
Democrats   = 222

Wisconsin (10), Georgia (16), Arizona (11), Pennsylvania (19), Michigan (15), and Nevada (6) have the remaining 77 electoral votes. In 2020, Democrats won all six of these states. This sweep is not so likely to occur in 2024.

Wisconsin (WI) and **Pennsylvania (PA)** have the same state voting records since 2000. Both states have elected moderate Democratic governors since 2022. Toni Evers was re-elected in Wisconsin, and Joshua Shapiro, a progressive Democrat, succeeded Democrat Governor Thomas Wolf in Pennsylvania in 2023. In 2022, Pennsylvania elected liberal Democrat John Fetterman to join Democrat Bob Casey as the state's U.S. senators.

Wisconsin and Pennsylvania have voted for the Democratic presidential candidate each year, except in 2016, when Trump won both states by narrow margins. The author's prediction for 2024 is that the 29 electoral votes for Wisconsin and Pennsylvania will follow the parties of their governors and their parallel histories.

Republicans	239		= 239
Democrats	222	+ 10 (**WI**) + 19 (**PA**)	= 251

Georgia's (GA) governors have been Republicans since 2003. Brian Kemp, the incumbent Republican Governor, was re-elected by a large margin in 2022. Democrats' U.S. Senate victories in Georgia in 2020 were historic and by small margins. In 2020 and 2022, there were runoff Senate elections that gave Democrats majority control of the U.S. Senate, but the Georgia Republican Senate candidates were not highly regarded or supported by sophisticated voters (One was a football player who never earned a college degree and a friend of Trump's.) The 2024 presidential race in Georgia is expected to be highly contested.

Arizona (AZ) is likely to return to its tradition of supporting Republican leaders (McCain, Goldwater), although the Governor and both U.S. Senators are Democrats. The ballot in Arizona will likely include proposed changes to a woman's right to choose. The composition of the voting public continues to change with the arrival of conservative voters, who have relocated from Southern California and are searching for a particularly favorable tax environment.

Recent changes in the state's voting regulations and the prohibition of private insurance to cover abortions indicate a continuing philosophical trend in Arizona. Moreover, the Arizona

State Supreme Court ruled in April 2024 that an antiquated bill that prohibited abortions is still enforceable.

```
Republicans  239  + 16 (GA) + 11 (AZ)   =  266
Democrats    251                         =  251
```

Michigan (MI) is forecast to be a victory for Democrats by a small margin. Data from the Michigan spring primary illustrate the state's competitiveness in November. Neighbor and Democratic Vice Presidential candidate Tim Walz is popular throughout most of the Midwest,

Governor Gretchen Whitmer strongly supports Vice President Harris, and Michigan re-elected the Governor by a near landslide in 2022. Years ago, the Governor testified in front of the Michigan legislature that she was raped as a college student and that if she had become pregnant, the option for an abortion would have been critical for her. Michigan allows abortion at any time during a pregnancy.

The state unified behind the Governor after eight ultra-right conservatives attempted to kidnap her. Since 2000, Democrats won Michigan's popular vote in 5 of the 6 presidential elections, losing to Trump by only 0.2 percent in 2016. A woman candidate for president could be a unique opportunity for Democrats to link with the Governor and Michigan voters on the issue of choice.

```
Republicans                  =  266
Democrats    251 + 15(MI)    =  266
```

Nevada (NV) is forecast to favor Harris and Walz in a close election to repeat 2020 and 2016. The late, Senate majority leader, Harry Reid's voter turnout system continues to operate effectively. Nevada's U.S. Senators are both Democrats and 3 of its 4 members of the House of Representatives are Democrats. In 2022, a Republican was elected Governor by a narrow margin. Democrats occupy 24 of the 42 state house seats and 12 of the 21 state senate seats. In the June Republican primary for the U.S. Senate, Trump supported the more conservative candidate, who received only 44 percent of the vote versus his more liberal

Republican opponent's 56 percent of the vote. Some of the 56 percent may be Republicans who will vote for Harris and Walz.

Adding Nevada's six electoral votes to the Democrats' total provides the 2024 Electoral College forecast:

Republicans: 266	=	266
Democrats: 266 + 6 (**NV**)	=	272

This is the same Electoral College forecast the author presented in January 2023 (Walker, 2023).

IMMEASURABLES AND UNPREDICTABLES

Every US presidential election will have immeasurable and unpredictable events.

In 2020, several states employed new voting equipment, but COVID-19 delayed or eliminated proper training with new technology and support for poll workers.

For 2024, the Democrats changed playerd, positions, and strategies.

Record numbers of young people voted in 2020. Federal Reserve policies and the U.S. economy are difficult to predict six months into the future; however, the Federal Reserve has indicated it will probably reduce target rates by a modest amount in the fall of 2024.

Other immeasurable effects include the full impact of a woman leading the Democratic ticket, women's vote affected by choice, inflation trends, latent effects of COVID-19, developments in the Israel – Hamas War, and Trump is continuing to face major trials after his September sentencing in New York. In addition, it is reported that Republican Party organizations are in chaos in several important states.

Candidates' Health: The health of either candidate could be compromised by the physical demands of a highly competitive campaign. Undiscovered background information may be discovered. Recall Thomas Eagleton, George McGovern's vice president-designate.

Trump's Health: Donald Trump is 78 years old and appears in good physical condition. He is overweight. Trump is recuperating from the assassination attempt on his life on July 13. His doctors say he is recovering well.

His claims as a candidate are not what democracy supports. He claims he wants to be a dictator, and he wants a tribunal to prosecute Liz Cheney. Many of his statements at his rallies and during his address at the Republican convention were false, outrageous, and unbalanced.

Harris Health: Kamala Harris is 59 years old and appears to be in excellent health with a balanced perspective for the life of a politician. The election is three months away.

Tables 7.4, 7.5, 7.6, and 7.7 show potential scenarios that should not be ignored. Table 7.4 shows the potential for a tie in the Electoral College, in which case Trump would become president.

JOE BIDEN'S LEGACY

Since 1973, Joe Biden has campaigned as a Democrat for national office, except for the four years following January 2013, after finishing his term as vice president. For November 2020, the Democrats prevailed on him to challenge incumbent Donald Trump for his re-election. Biden had planned to retire to his house in Rehoboth Beach, Delaware and drive his red Corvette. By 2019, he arranged for a national speaking tour, writing his memoirs, joining corporate boards for ethical firms, and affiliating with a research institute at the University of Pennsylvania.

When Democratic leaders recognized that Trump was likely to win a second term in 2020, they urged Biden to enter the race. Biden campaigned that his Administration would reestablish U.S. global relationships, participate actively in NATO, and improve American trade relationships with Europe and Asia.

Biden campaigned openly that he would propose legislation to increase personal and corporate taxes. He argued that Americans earning more than $400,000 per annum should pay higher taxes. The additional federal revenue was essential to pay for some the huge government costs that COVID-19 had thrust on lower income Americans. Many had lost their jobs, had no health insurance, and received no unemployment benefits when businesses and schools closed to stop the spread of the virus.

For 2024, Biden began a vigorous campaign while his opponents claimed he was too old, at age 81, and could not govern for four more years. He seemed frail, but his State of the Union address on March 27 convinced the nation he could serve another term.

The age issue surfaced again on June 27 when Biden debated Donald Trump. Listeners recognized that Biden was not thinking clearly, lost his train of thought, and made irrelevant statements on subjects that were not being discussed.

Biden continued to claim he would defeat Trump, who was recovering from an assassination attempt on his life. Many Democrats feared that the 2024 election would be disastrous for candidates for national, state, and local offices, even in situations where Democrats usually win easily. Biden refused to withdraw until party leaders, Senators, Congressmen, Congresswomen, major office holders, and friends convinced him to do so. He ended his campaign on July 21 and gave his total support to his vice president, Kamala Harris. She raised more than $100 million new campaign funds in the next 24 hours. Some of which was probably to honor President Biden for having the courage to make the right decision for the party and the nation.

The Biden Administration provides Kamala Harris with a good campaign foundation. In three and a half years, the Administration passed legislation to re-vitalize the economy and to disprove prognosticators who predicted a major 2023-2024 recession. The economy has regained its vitality. Employment is at full employment. Interest rates and housing prices are declining gradually. Inflation is at three percent for 2024, six percent below its peak during the Administration.

The Democratic Party owes Joe Biden tremendous gratitude for his many years of service, his victory in the 2020 campaign, and his 2022 leadership to recapture control of the House of Representatives.

Professor Ray Fair's forecasts since 1978 will be tested again this year. He claims the performance of the U.S. economy for approximately six-months before a presidential election usually determines whether the incumbent party is re-elected.

CONCLUSIONS

Popular Vote

The Democrats' 2024 popular vote was forecast to be 52.7 percent on December 1, 2022. It is revised as of August 6, 2024, after updates to the data. **Democrats are predicted to win 51.8 percent of the popular vote in November.** It is assumed that no independent candidate influences a single state's Electoral Vote. Robert F. Kennedy, Jr. is appealing to approximately 7 percent of the voters in some states, but this interest is waning as voters learn more about him.

Electoral College

The Democrats are forecast to win the Electoral College with 272 votes, including Nevada's 6 Electoral Votes. The possibility that the Electoral College could be tied is delineated in the Appendix and Table 7.4. If no candidate has a majority of the electors, the House of Representatives will select Trump to become president because 25 of the current Congressional delegations in the House have a majority of Republicans.

Many, perhaps a majority of voters, express dissatisfaction with their 2024 expected election choices. Numerous polls and focus groups suggest that neither party should nominate their presumed candidate. Replacing President Biden with Vice President Harris and adding Governor Walz as the candidate for vice president gives the Democrats a new, unexpected opportunity to challenge the Republicans.

APPENDIX - A

<u>1824</u>

The 2024 presidential election could repeat an experience that occurred 100 years ago. In 1824, the House of Representatives selected John Quincy Adams to become the sixth president. Andrew Jackson received 99 Electoral College votes, John Quincy Adams received 84, Henry Clay received 31, and Secretary of State William Crawford received 4. Since no candidate had a majority, the Constitution's 12th Amendment specifies that the House elects the president from among the three leading candidates. Henry Clay supported John Quincy Adams, who won and appointed Clay as Secretary of State.

<u>2024</u>

If the electoral vote is tied or no candidate has a majority of the votes, the House of Representatives will choose Trump. He would be chosen because 25 of the 2024 House delegations have a majority of Republicans, and two of the delegations have an equal number of Republicans and Democrats. (Table 7.4).

Table 7.5. shows one-way Harris can be elected and Table 7.6 shows one-way Trump can win. The slightest unforeseen incident or unexpected occurrence could dramatically change the author's forecasted Electoral College vote.

TABLE 7.1: DEMOCRATIC 2024 POPULAR VOTE MODEL
(December 1, 2022)

VARIABLE	DEFINITION	VALUE	COEFFICIENT (t-statistic)
CONSTANT	INTERCEPT	1.0	53.6561 (39.43)*
INFLATION	ANNUAL INFLATION	5.5	-0.8804 (-5.84)*
INCUMBENT	INCUMBENT RUNNING No = 0, Yes = 1	1.0	5.6844 (5.12)*
CANDID	CANDIDATES NOMINATED	5	-0.4761 (-4.65)*
DURATION	NUMBER OF TERMS INCUMBENT SERVED	1	-3.7824 (-3.75)*
WAR	COUNTRY AT WAR No =0, Yes =1	0	2.3724 (1.71)#
REP. PRES.	REPUBLICAN OCCUPIES WHITE HOUSE: No =0, Yes =1	0	2.6811 (1.85)#
CONTROL	DID PARTY CONTROLLING HOUSE CHANGE @ t-2 No = 0, Yes = 1	1	3.9890 (3.55)*
AR(1)	FORECAST ERROR CORRECTION	2.0040	-0.4394 (-1.94)#
R-SQ/ ADJ. R-SQ			0.81 / 0.74
F STAT / DW			11.43 / 2.24
2024 DEMOCRATIC PREDICTED POPULAR VOTE			53.70
*SIGNIFICANT AT THE .01 LEVEL + SIGNIFICANT AT THE .05 LEVEL # SIGNIFICANT AT THE .10 LEVEL			

TABLE 7.3: 2024 FORECASTS FOR 7 CRUCIAL STATES

STATE	2020% DIFFERENCE	2020 WINNER	2024 VOTES	ELECTORAL 2024 FORECAST		
				PARTY	CHOICE	REP FOR
MICHIGAN	2.80%	D	15	D	7	-3.11
NEVADA	2.40%	D	6	D	5	-2.62
WISCONSIN	0.60%	D	10	D	5	-1.40
PA	0.40%	D	19	D	5	-0.11
GEORGIA	0.20%	D	16	R	3	+5.77
N.CAROLINA	1.30%	R	16	R	3	+7.14
ARIZONA	0.40%	D	11	R	1	+9.02

TABLE 7.4: TIE ELECTORAL VOTES

	REP		DEM
AZ	11	MICH	15
NC	16	GA	16
PA	19	WIS	10
		NEV	6
SUM	46	SUM	47
*	223	*	222
ELEC. COL.	269	ELEC. COL.	269

TABLE 7.5: DEMOCRATS WIN PRESIDENCY

	REP		DEM
GA	16	PA	19
NC	16	MICH	15
AZ	11	WIS	10
		NEV	6
SUM	43	SUM	50
*	223	*	222
ELEC. COL.	266	ELEC. COL.	272

TABLE 7.6: REPUBLICANS WIN PRESIDENCY			
	REP		*DEM*
GA	16	PA	19
NC	16	MICH	15
AZ	11	WIS	10
NEV	6		
SUM	49	SUM	44
*	223	*	222
ELEC.	272	ELEC. COL.	266

TABLE 7.7: NEVADA, NEVADA, NEVADA (6)			
	REP		*DEM*
GA	16	PA	19
NC	16	MICH	15
AZ	11	WIS	10
SUM	43	SUM	44
*	223	*	222
ELEC. COL.	266	ELEC. COL.	266

* Initial Electoral College Allocation before 7 Swing States

REFERENCES

Abramowitz, Alan. (2020). "A Coronavirus Recession Could Doom Trump's Reelection Chances," Sabato's Crystal Ball, Center for Politics, University of Virginia.

Abramowitz, Alan. (2018). "Will Democrats Catch a Wave? The Generic Ballot Model and the 2018 US House Elections," *P.S.: Political Science & Politics,* 51(S1):4-6.

Abramowitz, Alan. (2016). "Will Time for Change Mean Time for Trump?" *P.S.: Political Science & Politics* Vol. 49(4). October, pp. 6, Alan I., (2008), "Forecasting the 2008 Presidential election with the Time-for-Change Model," P.S. Political Science and Politics, October.

Alesina, A. (1988), "Credibility and Policy Convergence in a Two-party System with Rational Voters," *American Economic Review,* 78:796-806.

Alesina, A. (1987). "Macroeconomics policy in a two-party system as a repeated game: *the Quarterly Journal of Economics,* 102, 6541-678.

American Bankers Association, (2010), "Dodd-Frank Wall Street Reform and Consumer Protection Bureau," Washington, DC. http://www.aba.com/RegReform/RR.ExecSummary.htm

Anderson, Nick and Susan Svrluga. (2021). "UNC-Chapel Hill Dramas Have Starkly Partisan Back Dramas," *The Washington Post, August 7*, p. A4.

Ardoin, Philip and Paul Gronke. (2016). "Forecasting the 2016 American National Elections," *P.S. Political Science & Politics,* 49(4). October.

Bafumi, Joseph, Robert S. Erikson, and Christopher Wliezien. (2018). "Forecasting the 2018 Midterm Election Using National Polls and District Information," *P.S.: Political Science & Politics,* 51(S1). October, pp. 7-11.

Bafumi, Joseph, Robert S. Erikson, and Christopher Wliezien. (2010). "Balancing, Generic Polls and Midterm Congressional Elections," *The Journal of Politics*, Vol. 72(3), July, pp. 705-719.

Baker, Peter and Susan Glasser (2022). *The Divider.* DoubleDay Press. New York, NY.

Baker, S. Bloom, N, Davis, S. (2016), "Measuring Economic Policy Uncertainty," *The Quarterly Journal of Economics*, 131, 1593-1636.

Balz, Dan (2021). "2020 Polls Suffered Worst Performance in Decades," *The Washington Post,* July 19, p. A2.

Berg, Joyce, Robert Forsythe, Forrest Nelson, Thomas Rietz, (2004), "Results from a Dozen Years of Election Futures Markets Research," The Handbook of Experimental Economic Results, C. Plott and V.L. Smith, eds., Elsevier Science B.V., Amsterdam, The Netherlands.

Boussalis, Constantine, Travis G. Coin, and Panna Patel. (2011). "The Political Consequences of Natural Disaster: A Cross-National Empirical Analysis," presented to the 52nd Annual Meeting of the International Studies Association, 16-19 March.

Bowen, Mark & Matthew Teague, (2022). "The Steal," Atlantic Monthly Press, New York, NY.

Box, George E. P. & Gwilym M. Jenkins. (1970). *Time Series Analysis forecasting and control.* Holden-Day. San Francisco.

Bureau of Economic Analysis. (2021). National Income and Product Accounts, Gross Domestic Product, 2nd Quarter 2021. U.S. Department of Commerce.

Bureau of Economic Analysis. (2016). National income and product accounts, gross domestic product, 3rd quarter 2016. U.S. Department of Commerce. July.

Bureau of Economic Analysis. (2013). National income and product accounts, gross domestic product, 3rd quarter 2013. U.S. Department of Commerce. July.

Bureau of Economic Analysis, (2012), "National Income and Product Accounts, Gross Domestic Product, 2nd Quarter 2012," U.S. Department of Commerce, July 27.

Caldwell, Leigh Ann and Liz Goodwin. (2024). "Warner To Marshal Senate Democrats to Ask Biden To Ask Biden to Exit race, Sources Say," *Wall Street Journal.* June 30, page A4.

Campbell, James, E. (2018). "The Seats-in-Trouble Forecasts of the 2018 Midterm Congressional Elections," *P.S.: Political Science & Politics*, 51(S1), October.

Campbell, James E. (2016). "The Trial-Heat and Seats-in-Trouble Forecasts of the 2016 Presidential and Congressional Elections," *P.S.: Political Science & Politics.* 49(4):664-668.

Campbell, James, E. (2013a). "The Miserable Presidential Election of 2012: A First Party-Term Incumbent Survives." *The Form.* 10, (4) 20=-28.

Campbell, J.E. (2013b). "Recap: forecasting the 2012 election," *P.S.:Political Science and Politics*, 46, (1), 40-41.

Campbell, James E. (2012). "Forecasting the Presidential and Congressional Elections of 2012. The Trial –Heat and the Seats-in-Trouble Models," *P.S.: Political Science & Politics,* 45(4):630-634.

Campbell, James E. and Michael S. Lewis-Beck. Editors, (2008). "US Presidential Election Forecasting," *International Journal of Forecasting,* Special Issue. Vol. 24(2) April-June.

Campbell, James E., (2008), "An Exceptional Election: Performance, Values, and Crisis in the 2008 Presidential Election, The Forum, The Berkeley Electronic Press, December.

Campbell, James E., (2004a), "The Fundamentals in U.S. Presidential Elections: Public Opinion, the Economy, and Incumbency in the 2004 Presidential Election," September, University of Buffalo, Buffalo, NY.

Campbell, James E., (2004b), "Forecasting the Presidential Vote in 2004: Placing Preference Polls in Context," *P.S.: Political Science and Politics*, October.

Campbell, James E., (2004c), "Introduction – The 2004 Presidential Election Forecasts," *P.S. Political Science and Politics,* October.

Campbell, J. E. and J. C. Garand, eds. (2000). *Before the Vote: Forecasting American National Elections*, Sage Publications, and Thousand Oaks, CA.

Campbell, James E., (2000), The American Campaign: U.S. Presidential Elections and Campaigns and the National Vote, Texas A & M Press, College Station, Texas.

Campbell, James E. (1997). "The Presidential Pulse and the 1994 Midterm Congressional Elections," *The Journal of Politics*, 59(3):830-857.

Campbell, James E., (1996), "Polls and Votes: The Trial Heat Presidential Election Forecasting Model, Certainty and Political Campaigns," American Politics Quarterly, October.

Campbell, James E. (1991). "The Presidential Surge and its Midterm Decline in Congressional Elections 1868-1988," *The Journal of Politics*, 53(2):477-487.

Campbell, James E. and Kenneth A. Wink, (1990), "Trial Heat Forecasts of the Presidential Vote," *American Politics Quarterly*, July.

Campbell, James E. (1985). "Explaining Presidential Loses in Midterm Congressional Elections," *The Journal of Politics*, 47(1):1140-1157.

Cambon, Sarah Chaney. (2022). "Economy Grows Amid Risks," *Wall Street Journal.* October 21, page A1+.

Carlton, Jim and Sigman Hughes. (2022). "Republicans See and Opening in Nevada Elections," *Wall Street Journal.* October 27, page A4.

Clement, Scott, Emily Guskin, Amy B. Wang and Sabrina Rodriguez. (2022). "A Double-Digit Dip in Democrats' Edge with Hispanics" *The Washington Post, October 16*, p. A16-A17.

Ceaser, James W. and Daniel DiSalvo, (2008), "The Magnitude of the 2008 Democratic Victory: By the Numbers, *The Forum, The Berkeley Electronic Press, December.*

Congressional Quarterly Inc. (1994, 2001). *Guide to U.S. Elections*,3ʳᵈ and 4th eds., Washington, DC.

CNN Politics. 2016, "Exit Polls," November 23.

Czasonis, Megan, Mark Kritzman, and David Turkington. (2021). "The Past as a Prologue: A New Approach to Forecasting," MIT Sloan Research Paper No. 6166-20.

DaSart, Jay A. (2020). "A Long-Range State-Level Forecast of the 2020 Presidential Election," *P.S..Political Science & Politics,* 53(4). October 15.

Dassonnville, Ruth and Charles Tien. (2020). "Introduction to Forecasting the 2020 US Elections," *.P.S. Political Science & Politics,* 53(4). October 15.

Dickerson, John. (2020). *The Hardest Job in the World.* Random House. New York, NY

Dmitrieva, Katia. (2019). "Trump's Re-Election Likely If Economy Stays on Course," Bloomberg, November 3.

Duehren, Andrew, Ken Thomas, and Natalie Andrews. (2021). "President Pitches Restamped $1.85 Spending Plan," *The Wall Street Journal, October 29*, page A1.

Duehren, Andrew. (2021). "Democrats Split on Tax Rate Changes," *The Wall Street Journal,* April 29, page A4.

Encyclopedia Britannica. (2024). "History & Society: The Iraq War, 2003 – 2011."

Enns, Peter K. and Julius Lagodny. (2020). "Forecasting the 2020 Electoral College Winner: The State Presidential Approval/State Economy Model," *P.S. Political Science & Politics,* 53(4). October 15.

Erikson, Robert S. and Christopher Wlezien. (2014).*The 2012 Campaign and the Timeline of Presidential Elections.* Chicano, IL. University of Chicago Press.

Erikson, Robert S. and Christopher Wlezien. (2012). "The Timeline of Presidential Elections," Chicago Studies in American Politics, University of Chicago.

Erikson, Robert S., (2009), "The American Voter and the Economy, 2008,*" P.S. Political Science and Politics,* July.

Erikson, Robert S. and Christopher Wlezien. (2008). "Are Political Markets Superior to Polls as Election Predictors?" *Public Opinion Quarterly*, 72(2):190-215.

Fair, Ray C. (2024a). Fair Model – Polly Vote. pollyvote.com/end/components/models/retrospective/fair-model

Fair, Ray C. (2024b). Compute Your Own Projections, April 29. https://fairmodel.econ.yale.edu/vote2020/index2.htm.

Fair, R.C. (2009a). "Interpreting the Predictive Uncertainty of Elections," *Journal of Politics*, 71(2):612-626.

Fair, R.C. (2009b). "Presidential and Congressional Vote-Share Equations," *American Journal of Political Science*, 53(1):55-72.

Fair, Ray C., (2008). "The Effect of Economic Events on Votes for President: 2008 Update," http://fairmodel.econ.yale.edu/vote2008/computev.htm

Fair, Ray C., (2004). "The Effect of Economic Events on Votes for President: 2000 Update," http://fairmodel.econ.yale.edu/vote2004/computev.htm

Fair, R.C. (2002). *Predicting Presidential Elections and Other Things*, Stanford University Press, Stanford, CA.

Fair, R.C. (1996). "Econometrics and Presidential Elections," *The Journal of Economic Perspectives*, 10(3):89-102.

Fair, R.C. (1978). "The Effect of Economic Events on Votes for President," *Review of Economics and Statistics*, 60(2):159-173.

Faris, David. (2020). "Time to Fight Dirty," *The* Week. April 4.

Farrell, Maurice. L., (1972. "The Dow Jones Averages, 1885 – 1970," Dow Jones & Company, New York City.

Ferri, Michael, (2008). "The Response of U.S. Equity Values to the 2004 Presidential Election," *Journal of Applied Finance*, Spring/Summer.

Federal Reserve Bank of Philadelphia. (2012, 2021, 2022, 2024). Quarterly Surveys of Professional Forecasters. Philadelphia, PA.

Federal Reserve Bank of St. Louis. (2018). FRED database.

Forsythe, R., Nelson, F., Neumann, G.R. & Wright J. (1992). Anatomy of an Experimental Political Stock Market. *American Economic Review*, 82, (5), 1142-1161.

Fowler, J. H., (2006a)." Elections and Markets the Effect of Partisanship, Policy Risk, and Electoral Margins on the Economy": *The Journal of Politics*. 68:89-103."

Fowler, J. H., (2006b). Altruism and Turnout". *The Journal of Politics*. 68(3):674-683.

Gaby, Max. (2011). "Impacts of TARP on Commercial Banks," *Journal of Applied Finance,* fall.

Goldfarb, Sam and Anthony DeBarros. (2024a). "Economic Forecasters See Good Times Ahead," *The Wall Street Journal,* April 15, Page A2.

Goldfarb, Sam and Anthony DeBarros. (2024b). "How Economists' Views Have Shifted," *The Wall Street Journal,* April 18, Page A2.

Goodell, J., Vahamaa S., (2013). "U.S. Presidential Elections and Implied Volatility: The role of Political Uncertainty," *Journal of Banking and Finance*, 37, 1108-1117.

Gramlich, Edward M. (2007). *Subprime Mortgages.* The Urban Institute. Washington, D.C.

Greenbaum, Stuart I., Anjan V. Thakor, and Arnoould W. A. Boot. (2016). *Contemporary Financial Intermediation.* 3rd. ed. Academic Press. New York.

Grier, K.B. and J. P. McGarrity. (2002). "Presidential Party, Incumbency, and the Effects of Economic Fluctuations on House Elections, 1916-1996," *Public Choice*, 110(1-2): 143-162.

Hamilton, A. (1788). Federalist Papers: No. 68. March 12. (http://avalon.law.yale.edu/18th_century/fed68.asp.

Helderman, Roseland S. (2021). "Arizona ballot report affirms Biden win and lack of Fraud," *The Washington Post.* September 25, Page A1.

Helfand, Zach. (2022). "Saudi Money and Donald Trump Roil the Game." *The New Yorker. October 24,* pp. 24 – 30.

Hibbs, Douglas A., Jr. (2012a). "The Bread and Peace Model: 2012 Presidential Postmortem," *PS: Political Science and Politics.* January, p. 41.

Hibbs, D.A. (2012b). "Obama's Reelection Prospects under 'Bread and Peace' Voting in the 2012 US Presidential Election," *P.S. Political Science and Politics,* 45, (4), 635-639.

Hibbs, Douglas A., Jr. (2000). "Bread and Peace Voting in U.S. Presidential Elections," *Public Choice.* 104:149-180.

Hogan, Larry. (2024). "Project 2025 shreds American values," *The Washington Post,* July 21, p. A24.

Holbrook, Thomas M. (2009). "Economic Considerations and the 2008 Presidential Election," .*P.S. Political Science and Politics,* 42(2):473-478.

Hsu, Spencer S. (2024). "Charges Revised in Jan. 6 cases," *The Washington Post, July 17*, pages B1, B2.

Jacobson, Gary C., (2009), "The 2008 Presidential and Congressional Elections," PSQ, Spring.

James, Chandler. (2022). "Does President Trump's Outrageous Behavior Work? Results from Two Randomized Controlled Trials. *Presidential Studies Quarterly.* 52(2): 411-428.

Jennings, Will, Michael S. Lewis-Beck, and Christopher Wlezien. (2020). "Election forecasting: too far out?" *International Journal of Forecasting.* 36(23);949-962.

Jens, C.E., (2017), "Political Uncertainty and Investment: Causal Evidence from U.S. Gubernatorial Elections, *Journal of Financial Economics*, 124, 563-579.

Kelly, B. Pastor, L., Veronesi, P., (2016), "The Price of Political Uncertainty: Theory and Evidence from the Option Market," *The Journal of Finance,* 71, 2417 – 2480.

Kramer, Gerald H. (1971). "Short-Term Fluctuations in U.S. Voting Behavior," *American Political Science Review:* 65(1): 131-143.

Lahart, Justin (2024). "Benefits of Tight Job Market Now at Risk," *Wall Street Journal. August 5, p. A2.*

Lemire, Jonathan (2022). *The Big Lie.* Flatiron Books. New York, NY.

Lewis-Beck, Michael S. and Charles P. Tien.(2023). "Economic, COVID, and Election Forecast: Did Trump Escape," *American Political Research.* 51(5):619-622.

Lewis-Beck, Michael S. and Charles P. Tien. (2018). "House forecasts: Structure-X Models for 2018," *PS: Political Science & Politics,* 51(S1):pp. 7-11.

Lewis-Beck, Michael and Charles Tien. (2016). "The Political Economy Model: 2016 US Election Forecasts," *PS: Political Science & Politics* Vol. 49(4):661-663.

Lewis-Beck, M.S. with Nadeau, R. & Belanger, E. (2013). Economics and Elections Revisited, *Comparative Political Studies,* 46, (5), 551-573.

Lewis-Beck, Michael S., (2009), "The Economy, Obama, and the 2008 Election," *P.S. Political Science and Politics,* July.

Lewis-Beck, Michael S. and Richard Nadeau, (2009). "Obama, and the Economy in 2008," *P.S. Political Science and Politics,* July.

Lewis-Beck, M.S. (2006). "Does Economics Still Matter? Econometrics and the Vote," *Journal of Politics*, 68(1):208-212.

Lewis-Beck, Michael S., (2001a), "Modelers v. Pollsters: The Election Forecasts Debate," The Harvard International Journal of Press/Politics, Spring.

Lewis-Beck, Michael S. and Charles Tien, (2001b), "Election 2000: How Wrong was the Forecast?" *American Politics Research*, May.

Lewis-Beck, M. S. and M. Paldam, (2000a), "Economic Voting: An Introduction,"

Electoral Studies, June/September.

Lewis-Beck, Michael S. and Charles Tien, (2000b), "The Future in Forecasting: Prospective Presidential Models," in J.E. Campbell and J. C. Garand (eds.), (2000), Before the Vote: Forecasting American National Elections, Sage Publications, Thousand Oaks, CA.

Lewis-Beck, Michael S. and Tom W. Rice. (1992). *Forecasting Elections.* CQ Press. Washington, DC.

Lichtman, Allan J. (2016). *Predicting the Next President: The Keys to the White House 2016.* Rowman & Littlefield, New York, NY.

Linn, Susanna, Jonathan Moody, and Stephanie Asper, (2009), "Explaining the Horse Race of 2008," Obama, and the 2008 Election," *P.S. Political Science and Politics,* July.

Lepore, J. (2016). "How to steal an election," *The New Yorker,* July 4, pages 20 – 24.

Lucey, Catherine, Andrew Restuccia and Ken Thomas. (2024). "Incumbency Shifts Trump-Biden Dynamic," *Wall Street Journal,* February 3-4:A4.

Lucey, Catherine and Sabrina Siddiqui. (2021). "President to Push Economic Agenda," *The Wall Street Journal,* April 29, pages A1, A4.

Lynch, David J. (2021). "Uneven fiscal recovery has rising prices, inflation risk," *The Washington Post,* May 11, pages A1, A18.

Lynch, G. Patrick. (2002). "Midterm Elections and Economic Fluctuations: The Response of Voters over Time," *Legislative Studies Quarterly*, 27(2):265-294.

Malkiel, Burton G., (2023). *A Random Walk Down Wall Street*, 12th ed., W. W. Norton Company. New York, N. Y.

Markus, Gregory B., (1992), The Impact of Personal and National Economic Conditions on Presidential Voting, 1956-1988," *American Journal of Political Science,* August.

Martin, Jonathan and Alexander Burns. (2022*). This Will Not Pass.* Simon and Schuster, New York, NY.

Matuz, R. (2015). *The Presidents Fact Book Revised and Updated*, Black Dog & Leventhal Publishers, New York, N.Y.

Nadeau, Richard and Michael S. Lewis-Beck, (2001), "National Economic Voting in U.S. Presidential Elections," *The Journal of Politics*, February.

Nagar, V., Schoenfeld, J. and Wellman, (2017). "Economic Policy Uncertainty and Information Asymmetry," University of Utah, working paper.

NBER. National Bureau of Economic Research.*US Business Cycle Expansions and Contractions.* (2024). Business Cycle Data. July 19.

Norpoth, Helmut. (2020). "Primary Model Predicts Trump Victory,*" P.S. Political Science & Politics* Vol. 54(4):63-66.

Norpoth, Helmut. (2016). "Primary Model Predicts Trump Victory," *P.S. Political Science & Politics* 49(4):655-658.

Norpoth, Helmut. (1996). "Of Time and Candidates: A Forecast for 1996," *American Politics Research*. Vol. 24(4):443-467.

Olorunnipa, Toluse. (2024). "Biden Exits Race," *The Washington Post,* July 22, p. A1,A13.

Ord, Keith. & Robert Fildes. 2013. *Principles of Business Forecasting.* South-Western Cengage Learning. New York.

Powell, G. Bingham, Jr. and Guy D. Whitten, (1993), "A Cross-National Analysis of Economic Voting: Taking Accounting of the Political Context," *American Journal of Political Science,* May.

Prokop, Andrew. (2021). "Composition of the Electorate By Race, 2008 – 2020," *Catalist* May 10.

Reitz, Thomas A., Joyce Berg, Forrest Nelson, and Robert Forsythe (2020). "The (Re) Election of 2020: Current Events and Historical Perspectives from the Iowa Electronic Market," *P.S.: Political Science* 53(4). October 15.

Remnick, D. (2016). "It happened here," *The New Yorker,* November 28, pages 54 – 65.

Reston, Maeve. (2024). "In Nevada, Democrats Pion Hopes on Abortion Message," *The Washington Post, June 12,* pp. A13, A20.

Rucker, Hannah. (2020). "A Closer Look at How Latinos Voted in Texas for the 2020 Election," *Vote Texas,* November 4.

Salcedo, Andrea (2021). "DeSantis offers $5,000 to police who decline vaccines to relocate to Florida," *The Washington Post, October 26,* p. A8.

Santa-Clara, Pedro and Rossen Valkanov, (2003), "The Presidential Puzzle: Political Cycles and the Stock Market," *The Journal of Finance,* October.

Scherer, Michael. (2024). "Democrats look to Nebraska to shore up Biden's blue wall," *The Washington Post.* February 19: A3.

Schiff, Adam. (2022). *Midnight in Washington.* Random House. New York, NY.

Silver, Nate. (2016). "Models Based on 'Fundamentals' Have Failed at Predicting Presidential Elections," *The New Times,* March 26.

Silver, Nate. (2012a). The Signal and the Noise: Why So Many Predictions Fail - but Some Don't," The Penguin Press, New York, NY.

Silver, N. (2012b). Nate Silver 538 Blog: Why NYT pollster is right about election 2012.

References

http://www.policymic.com/articles/18098/nate-silver-538-blog-why-nyt-pollster-is-right-about-election-2012, November 1, 12:53 AM ET.

Sorkin, Andrew Ross. (2019) *Too Big To Fail: The Inside Story of How Wall Street and Washington Fought to Save the Financial System- and – Themselves.* Viking Press. New York City.

Sotomayor Marianna and Silva Foster-Frau. (2022). "Florida Serves As Alarm for Democrats," *The Washington Post, October 16*, p. A1, A18.

Stigler, George, J. (1973). "General Economic Conditions and National Elections," *American Economic Review, 63*(5):160-167.

Suro, Roberto (2022). "Why the Latino Vote Will Continue to Surprise Us for the Next 20 Years," *The Washington Post,* October 30, page A 27.

The Economist. (2024). "The Right to Choose," June 1, p. 12.

The Economist. (2024). Economic and Financial Indicators. July 20, p. 73.

The Economist. (2024). Economic and Financial Indicators. June 1, p. 73.

The Economist. (2022). Economic and Financial Indicators. numerous issues.

The Economist. (2017). Economic and financial indicators. January 21, p. 76.

Theil, Henri. (1966). *Applied Economic Forecasting.* North-Holland Publishing Company. Amsterdam.

Thomas, K., and A. Linskey. "Biden Forcefully Rejects Calls To Ditch His Re-Election Bid,". (2024). *Wall Street Journal.* July 6-7, A1,A4.

Thomas, K., S. Hughes, N. Andrews, G. Zuckerman. " Biden's Top Allies Urge Party to Stick with Him," (2024). *Wall Street Journal.* July 1, A1, A4.

Timiraos, Nick. (2024). "Market Selloff Set To test Fed Strategy," *Wall Street Journal.* August 6, pp. A1, A2.

Timiraos, Nick and Paul Kiertnan (2024). "Fed Faces Renewed Threat Of Hard Economic Landing," *Wall Street Journal.* August 5, A2.

Timiraos, Nick and David Uberti (2024). "Fed Sees Just One Rate Cut After Soft Inflation," *Wall Street Journal.* June 12, A1-A2.

Timiraos, Nick and David Uberti (2024). "Fed Sees Just One Rate Cut After Soft Inflation," *Wall Street Journal.* June 12, A1-A2.

Timiraos, Nick. (2022b). Fed Lifts Rate, Signals More," *The Wall Street Journal, September 22:*A1.

Timiraos, Nick. . (2022a). "Fed Lifts Rates, Signals 'Ways to Go.'" *Wall Street Journal.* November 3:A1-A2.

Timiraos, Nick. (2022b). Fed Lifts Rate, Signals More," *The Wall Street Journal, September 22:*A1.

Toobin, Jeffrey. (2020). "What Comes Next," *The New Yorker.* Sept. 28:34-43.

Torry, Harriet and Anthony DeBarros. (2022). "Recession Now Seen As More Likely," *The Washington Post, October 17:*A2.

Tufte, Edward R. (1975). "Determinants of the Outcomes of Midterm Congressional Elections," *American Political Science Review*, September:812-826.

Tully, Shawn. (2022). Fortune Interview with Larry Summers. September 23.

US Coronavirus Vaccine Tracker. (2021). *USA Facts,* October 3.

U.S. Government Printing Office. (2005). Statistics of the Presidential and Congressional Election of November 2004. Washington, DC.

U.S. Census. (2021). "Census Apportionment Results Released," April 26.

Viser, Matt (2024). "Defiant Biden: 'I am Running," *The Washington Post, July 6,* pp. A 1, A4.

Walker, David A. (2024). "Incumbency since the 1800s," Georgetown University, Washington, DC.

Walker, David A. (2023). "Forecasting the 2020 and 2024 U.S. Presidential Elections,"

Journal of Forecasting. 42(6):1519-1535.
Walker, David A. (2018).*Credit Unions' Acquisitions of Banks and Thrifts,* Westchester Publishing Services for the Filene Institute, Madison, Wisconsin, 2018.

Walker, David A. (2018). "How They Lost the Presidency," *Applied Economics*, March, 50(38): 4113-4121.

Walker, David. (2015). *Room To Grow: Credit Union Business Lending*, Kinetic Publishing Services for the Filene Institute, Madison, Wisconsin.

Walker, David A. (2013). "The 2012 U.S. Presidential Election: Did Markets Matter?" *Journal of Accounting and Finance*. 13(5), pp 49 -62.

Walker, David A. (2008). "Presidential Election Forecasts". *The Forum*, 6(4), article 6.

Walker, David A. (2006). "Predicting Presidential Election Results," *Applied Economics*, March 38(5):483-490.

Walker, David A. (1997). *Credit Union Insurance and Regulation*, principal investigator, Georgetown Business School, Center for Business-Government Relations, Georgetown University. *Wall Street Journal.* (2021). "Inflation Surge Rattles Markets," May 13:A1-A2.

Walters, Ryan S. (2022). "The Jazzage President," Regency History, Washington, DC

Washington Post. (2021). "First 100 Days," Special Section AA, April 28.

Washington Post. (2016). "Election 2016," section A, November 9.

Wlezien, C. and Erikson, R.S. (2002). "The Timeline of Presidential Election Campaigns," *The Journal of Politics*, 64, (4).

Wikipedia. (2021a). "2020 United States presidential election."

Wikipedia. (2021b). "List of current members of the House of Representatives," May 12.

Woodward, Bob and Robert Costa. (2021). *Peril.* Simon & Schuster, New York.

Wootson, Cleve R., Jr. and Tyler Pager. (2022). "Biden Focuses on Abortion in Democrats' Final sprint Before Midterms," *The Washington Post, October 19:*A7.

Yellen, Janet L. (2015). *Inflation Dynamics and Monetary Policy,* Philip Gamble Memorial Lecture, University of Massachusetts, Amherst, Amherst, MA, September 15.

Zambakari, Christopher. (2019). "Why Trump Does Not Need the Popular Vote to Retain the White House in 2020," The Fletcher Forum on World Affairs. Tufts University. Boston, MA.

Zitner, A, S. Hughes, N. Andrews. Down- Ballot Democrats Fret That Debate Could Cost Them," (2024). *Wall Street Journal.* July 1, A5.

Zitner, Aaron. (2024). "Voters' View of Economy Warm, Benefiting Biden Just Marginally," *Wall Street Journal,* March 4:p. A1.

Zitner, A. and A. DeBarros. (2022). "Republicans Make Inroads With Some Groups," *Wall Street Journal, November 21:p.* A4.

Zitner, Aaron. (2021). "Presidential Poll Miss Was Worst in 40 Years," *Wall Street Journal,* May 14: p.A3.

Zitner, A. (2016). "How two parties changed in 2016," *The Washington Post*, November 26, page A4.

www.realclearpolitics.com/epolls/2008/president/us, Real Clear Politics

www.fairmodel/econ.yale.edu/vote2012.index2

www.realclearpolitics.com/epolls/2008/president/us, Real Clear Politics

www.bea.gov/newsreleases/glance.htm

References

https:en.wikipedia.org/wiki/Household_income_in_the_United_
States

https:en.wikipedia.org/wiki/List_of_U.S._states_by_income

https:en.wikipedia.org/wiki/List_of_U.S._states_by_African-
American_population

https:en.wikipedia.org/wiki/List_of_U.S._states_by_Hispanic_and_
Latino_population

http:usinflationcalculator.com/inflation/historical-inflation-rates

https:en.wikipedia.org/wiki/List_of_current_United_States   -
governors

https://presidentialcampaignselectionsreference.wordpress.com/o
verviews/20th-century/1900-overview/.

http://www.thegreenpapers.com/P12/R

www.ingramcontent.com/pod-product-compliance
Lightning Source LLC
Chambersburg PA
CBHW020356270326
41926CB00007B/465